ARZAK + ARZAK

Grub Street • London

Preface

By Guille Viglione

From the baptism to the funeral, in the Basque Country all the major events take place around a table. People eat and drink, but also sing, play cards, build friendships and reach agreements. This is not an exaggeration. The day Juan Mari's father died, his widow, Paquita Arratibel, didn't get out of the kitchen. She made fish soup, red beans, hake in a green sauce and roasted chicken for sixty members of the family who had come from Ataun. It was 1951, Juan Mari was nine and Arzak was still a family eatery next to the state road.

Paquita spent her life glued to the stove. She started to cook when she was very young, in some summer visitors' house, and after that she raised the family offering wedding receptions at the tavern on the Miracruz hill; the same location where foodies from all around the world meet today. Nowadays being a chef means living a demanding life, but by the middle of the twentieth century kitchens looked like the core of a submarine: the properties weren't well aired and the coal stoves created a very suffocating atmosphere. It was probably because of this that Paquita made every effort to prevent her son from being a chef. She sent Juan Mari to Madrid for him to become a building engineer, but there are some roads you don't choose. They choose you.

In the seventies, Juan Mari convinced his mother to have a corner of the restaurant for himself. He started testing new recipes and served his customers the first creations of what soon became known as the New Basque Cuisine, a spontaneous movement started by a group of cooks that renovated Spanish cuisine and placed Donostia (San Sebastian) on the map of international cuisine.

In 1994, Elena Arzak started to work in the family kitchen, but by that time she was the veteran cook of a thousand stoves. After preparing herself in Switzerland for years, she developed professionally from her base in hotels, and later in the best kitchens of the world, from Troisgros to El Bulli. Juan Mari's daughter brings to completion the fourth generation of the family working in the restaurant business. From that point on, father and daughter made an unbreakable team that cooks, tastes, imagines and runs a four-handed family house.

Today Elena and Juan Mari's kitchen is the embodiment of what gastronomy means for the Basque people: a cultural value that goes beyond the simple act of eating. The Arzaks undertake research for an avant-garde cuisine and merges influences from all over the world, but they never lose touch with their Basque roots. Their secret is combining global modernity with the traditions of the Basque grandmothers, which shows respect for the inheritance they received and the identity of a people. With those premises traditional Basque cuisine has evolved while staying loyal to the original flavours. A recognisable and intense flavour that prioritises the source and seasonality of the produce.

It was 121 years ago when Elena's great-grandparents started this eatery. The family house has had three Michelin stars for thirty years now. The name Arzak shines in the list of The World's 50 Best Restaurants and in the most renowned guides in the world. But despite the awards and the pressure of being always at the top, Juan Mari and Elena are still loyal to the idea of a family restaurant. They don't work for the critics and they don't get obsessed with the rankings, because their first priority is to make their guests happy. Maybe that's their uniqueness. In Arzak they create, innovate and take risks, but they never forget their mission is to create happiness. Nothing makes sense if the customers don't leave the table with a smile.

On egin, which in the Basque language means bon appétit.

Introduction

By Gabriella Ranelli

«Vision is the art of seeing things that are invisible for other people.»

Jonathan Swift

Arzak has been a household name in Spain since the 1970s and Juan Mari Arzak, who presides over the family restaurant, is the innovative force behind its rise to the upper echelons in the world of culinary art. The restaurant, nestled in the heart of the Basque Country in Northern Spain, is a temple. He has cooked for everyone, from local families to royalty and luminaries like Bruce Springsteen and John Malkovich.

On the last night of my first visit to San Sebastian, the Belle-Époque city on the Bay of Biscay, I dined at Restaurante Arzak. It was August 22, 1987, and Arzak was the one place I really wanted to experience in this food obsessed city. It would be my first Michelin-starred restaurant and the one mentioned with reverence by everyone I'd met since I arrived in the country.

The evening began with fresh foie gras. Then came wild mushrooms and chervil wrapped in translucent sheets of pasta, grilled hake collar with a warm vinaigrette, and roasted squab. To finish, a warm mint chocolate dessert was served. Long-aproned waitresses whisked away plates and filled wine glasses with discretion. Caught up in the atmosphere and unaccustomed to long European dinners, I lost track of time and was bundled into a taxi and rushed to the train station just in time for the night train to Madrid. The seductive elegance of Arzak contrasted with my rumbling *couchette* as I replayed the evening.

That meal changed the course of my life. I left a future in the New York art world and moved to San Sebastian in 1989, the year Arzak garnered its third Michelin star.

I found a tiny flat near the market in *la parte vieja* – the old town – at a politically volatile time when Saturday's marketing or Friday's *aperitivo* was often interrupted by small riots. The bar owners would pull down their metal grates with the customers held captive inside. Momentarily imprisoned, we would wait out the siege eating vermouth-soaked olives and striking up conversations that aided my Spanish, which was already improving daily from talking to bartenders and market ladies.

My love affair with the local culture and its food continued as my cheesemonger, Aitor, showed me how to slice a wheel of Idiazabal properly and my friend Karmelo taught me how to filet a sole as he imparted the unwritten rules of belonging to that definitive Basque social group, the *cuadrilla*.

Juan Mari Arzak earned his first Michelin star in 1972, when the New York City restaurant industry – like the city itself – was in crisis. The health food craze was stirring, Alice Waters was leading a defining moment in California cuisine, and the rest of the country just wanted a good steak. *Nouvelle cuisine* was the talk of France and the first McDonald's opened in London. Spain, isolated by politics, was on the sidelines of the international food scene. But San Sebastian, just half an hour from the chic French resort of Biarritz, was starting to make waves.

Over the thirty years since I took that train, I've witnessed the development of Basque cuisine. I cooked in a few restaurants and many of the chefs became good friends over the course of countless late nights. As food journalists began to discover Spain, I became a liaison between the Basque food world and the English-speaking press. Since then pintxo bars on narrow side streets have become dining hot spots and kitchen apprentices have grown into renowned chefs.

In the 1990s, I started the first wine and food travel company in the Basque Country. I am proud to have been part of a small vanguard that helped bring Spain to international attention as a food and wine destination. As the political turmoil eased, intrepid visitors began to arrive – lured by articles in specialized food magazines – long before Instagram or the World's 50 Best Restaurants list, and certainly before anyone would call themselves a 'foodie'. In 2004 the legendary gourmand R.W. Apple came to San Sebastian and I was fortunate enough to show him around. His *New York Times* article was the beginning of a sea change. He wrote, "Arzak typifies the contemporary Basque culinary spirit – experimental, questing, hard to satisfy, but proudly, solidly anchored in local tradition." Suddenly the names of Basque chefs were on the lips of a much wider audience.

For nearly twenty years Juan Mari has shared the role of chef at Restaurante Arzak with his daughter Elena. The Arzaks are quintessentially Basque. They are humble, hardworking and loyal. Their pride in their country is evident as they champion the local producers – fishermen, cheesemakers, and farmers – who are the backbone of the Basque Country. Today, anchovies from the Cantabrian Sea, Txakoli wine and Idiazabal cheese can be found in Melbourne and Moscow. Cooking students, chefs and those travelling for a taste of something special have the Basque Country on their radar.

This book tells the story of a family and a cuisine, while marking a subtle passing of the torch. It takes a look at Juan Mari's role as a leader of the New Basque Cuisine movement, a cutting-edge chef and restaurateur, and an inspiration for generations of young cooks.

It also follows Elena's rise in the kitchen, recognizing the essence of her creative process and the magic she and her father create through the design and balance of plates and menus. This introduction to the close-knit team of visionaries and their innovative recipes offers a glimpse into the future of Restaurante Arzak.

Arzak is a family restaurant, and their extended family is broad. They look after their own, always ready to pick up the phone with congratulations or commiserations. Former staffers and *stagiers* stop by for advice or to catch up on news before the restaurant goes on holiday for two weeks every June and November. Whenever a local forager peeps around the open kitchen door with a basket of *boletus* mushrooms, he stays for a beer. A winemaker may bring a few bottles of his latest vintage and stay for an hour discussing its merits over a plate of ham at the bar.

As Juan Mari's translator for many years, I too have become part of the extended family. Perched on the catbird seat at the end of the bar, I set up my laptop, chat with the staff and wait for Elena to spare a minute between the dining room and her kitchen duties. Our work starts in the bar area and continues into the kitchen, where we discuss menu items over coffee and occasionally join the family or one of Juan Mari's many friends for lunch.

For more than a decade I've had the privilege to observe all the characters and movements involved in this carefully orchestrated family affair from the best seat in the house. It is my great honour to open the door and share their story.

1

Arzak-Enea

A father, a daughter and a Basque restaurant

Arzak-Enea, the House of Arzak, as it's known in Basque, is a solid four-storey brick building built in 1897. It sits on a rise at what was once the edge of San Sebastian, in a spot called *Alto de Vinagres*, or Vinegar Hill. On the other side of the hill is an industrial port, and a busy main road passes just a few metres from the front door. This building has been the site of Restaurante Arzak for more than 120 years. Here behind a recently installed zinc façade, the restaurant and its chef, Juan Mari Arzak, have been a driving force in transforming San Sebastian from a small resort city on the north coast of Spain into an international culinary mecca.

Arzak has held three Michelin stars, the maximum that can be awarded by the esteemed culinary guide, since 1989. It is a member of many of the world's most prestigious associations and appears in countless restaurant guides. It has also been ranked on the World's 50 Best Restaurant list since the ranking's early days.

Throughout its many years of service, Arzak's attention to detail and the courage to break taboos have won the chef and his restaurant a dizzying list of accolades; nevertheless, the restaurant holds its cards close to its chest. The dining rooms have a reserved elegance: decorum reigns, linens are crisp, and colours are muted. Each day shortly before service begins, the waitresses, in long grey aprons check place settings; the maitre d' reviews the reservations; and up to moments before the service begins, there is no handle on the front door. It cannot be opened from the outside until someone slips the handle back onto its metal spindle. As soon as that happens, the first guests begin to arrive and the dance begins.

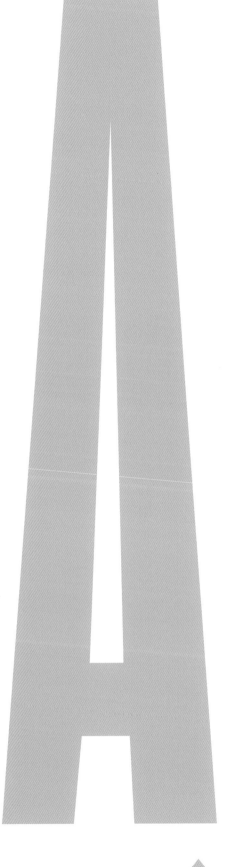

The quiet precision of the front of the house belies the buzz of activity behind the kitchen doors. A veritable maze of stairways, wine cellars and kitchens come alive like a beehive in spring. The final details of the cooks' *mise en place* are readied, and the team is set to go. Doors – eight in the reception area alone – open and close with the speed and coordination of a stage comedy. More doors swing open to various hidden rooms, offices, antechambers, and family apartments. (Yes, people live at Arzak!) The old house is in full motion.

Lunch is the main meal of the day in Spain, and service at Arzak begins at 1:45 pm, which is late by the standards of countries where food marks a pause in the workday, but very much on time in San Sebastian, where food is an occasion to celebrate.

The stream of guests on a typical day might include two German art collectors in town for a visit to Chillida Leku Sculpture Park, four American women celebrating a 50th birthday, a chic Chinese couple, and a young foursome, casual in the hip style that serves as identification no matter where they're from. An elegant Basque family arrives as well: the grandfather wearing a black beret, three identically dressed grandchildren and, in command of it all, their *Amona*, the grandmother, perfectly coiffed upon arrival at 2 pm. The family is seated with due deference by Kontxi Beobide, the long standing maitre d', but not before Juan Mari Arzak (still buttoning the last button of a freshly pressed chef's coat) emerges from behind a curtained glass door and crosses the reception area to greet the venerable *Amona* and her family. They'd gotten their driver's licenses together when they were teens and banter flirtatiously, causing the grandchildren to giggle.

Juan Mari's youngest daughter and co-chef is Elena Arzak. She's petite and confident in a crisp white apron, her hair in a high ponytail. Slipping out of the kitchen and over to the reservation desk, she does one last scan of the day's tables and then steps forward to greet the collectors in perfect German.

Mariano Rodriguez, the sommelier, greets a Riojan winemaker and his Belgian clients and escorts them to a small private dining room on the second floor. Kontxi tends to the Americans in the main dining room, and the Chinese couple request hot water with lemon while waiting for a tour of the kitchen. As the restaurant's fame has grown, procuring a reservation has become more difficult, and as the preparation of its complex cuisine has become more challenging, guests increasingly want a look at what goes on behind the scenes. Once unheard of, a visit to the kitchen, cellar, and laboratory has become a sought-after privilege for a lucky few.

Behind the curtained glass door to the kitchen, the silhouettes of two waitresses can be seen clearing the chef's table. Reserved for the Arzak family's midday meal, today a group of Spanish designers has been granted the prized vantage point for lunch. Like a kitchen tour, dining at the chef's table is a modern concept. The days of roaring fires and smoky kitchens have long passed, and many of today's diners want to see the chefs at work. Guests dining in the kitchen are served by waitresses assigned exclusively to their table, and they can watch every bit of the action going on behind the scenes. At Arzak, the chefs remain at their stations behind the pass, the long stainless-steel surface that acts as a barrier between the kitchen and the serving area.

The dance continues. A *stagier*, or kitchen apprentice, pops into the bar to fetch a bottle of tequila to flambé a new crab dish. Igor Zalakain, Juan Mari's right-hand man, who has taken the hip foursome up a back stairway on a route that passes through the wine cellar to the laboratory, now shepherds them down another flight of stairs to the door of the dining room, before disappearing through yet another door just as the maitre 'd appears to guide them to their table.

More guests arrive. More doors open and close. And then, suddenly, it's quiet in Juan Mari's and Elena's base camp: the front-of-the-house bar. While the dining room is bustling, the father-daughter duo can field interview questions, plan the upcoming week or review a conference presentation, in between trips to the kitchen and dining rooms. All of the rooms have their own doorways leading to other areas where more exchanges take place. Someone is always coming or going, some door is always swinging wide open. Before lunch, suppliers, friends, or messengers stop by with products, town gossip, or news about a wonderful new ceramicist. After lunch, it could be a journalist from Chicago, Japan, or the local paper coming for a cup of coffee and an interview.

As the lunch service settles into its natural rhythm, Juan Mari eases himself onto the small loveseat and surveys the pale grey room. Elena sits facing him, hopping up every so often to check on guests and to make sure everything is running smoothly in the kitchen. They speak in Spanish with an occasional aside in Basque, the ancient native language of the region. In public Elena refers to her father as Juan Mari, but here he is *Aita*, 'father' in Basque. The conversation ranges from gentle exchanges to the occasional flare-up of exasperation as each tries to make a point. Juan Mari likes to spin a story with his melodious voice while Elena immediately gets down to brass tacks. What may seem like a heated argument is usually a debate between chefs, rather than between father and daughter. There's always respect. When it comes to food, they are colleagues on equal footing and they understand each other.

The lunch service stretches into the late afternoon, which leaves little time for rest before the dinner guests begin to arrive at 8:45pm and the dance begins once again.

Each of them takes turns visiting tables during the long meals and they try to say goodbye to all their guests. With kind words and friendly smiles, they put first-time visitors at ease, catch up on news with regulars, and reminisce with long-time guests from all corners of the world. The family and staff know their patrons well, anticipate their needs, and thoughtfully choose the experiences that will most captivate them. The service is warm, the atmosphere is friendly, and the experience is one that many diners will enjoy again and again. The connections they make and the affection they have for their guests is important because *Arzak-Enea* is their home. At the core of it all, diners at the restaurant are guests in the Arzaks' house.

It's long past midnight when the dinner service ends. Juan Mari went home hours ago. Elena's now the one who stays until the end. At around 1:30 am, her cousin Ramón, the valet, removes the door handle from its spindle and lowers the shutter. Elena takes off her apron, folds it over the back of a chair, turns off the lights in the bar and slips out through the side door and into the night.

Though the building is no longer Juan Mari's actual residence, he was born in *Arzak-Enea* before hospital births became the norm in the sixties, and he insists that he has spent more time in the restaurant than in his own living room. Elena is well on her way to doing the same. The responsibility of carrying on a family tradition stretches back more than a century. Elena is the fourth generation to run this restaurant, and she's instilling the same sense of pride and duty in her own children, although it's too soon to tell if they will follow in her footsteps.

The Dining Room

Juan Mari and the history of Arzak

Juan Mari Arzak appears first in silhouette, behind the opaque sliding glass door to the kitchen, before he enters the dining room. A strong presence in a pristine chef's coat, with close-cropped white hair and eyes that twinkle behind this season's groovy yellow frames, he commands the room. He forgoes the long white apron these days since he no longer works the line. Now in his mid 70s, Juan Mari is settling into the role of patriarch. He drives the short route to the restaurant every day in his black SUV, and he still makes the rounds at La Bretxa market to visit with farmers and fishmongers or puts in an appearance as the head of the jury at a local cooking or cheese competition. But most of the time he is where he's always been: at the helm of the restaurant where he was born.

Frosted glass windows separate the bustling street outside from the ground floor dining room, which straddles the old and the new. The all-female wait staff wear long grey pinafore aprons as they glide between tables. The walls are lined with concrete sculptures embedded with antique silverware moulds created just for the restaurant. A dark grey Catellani & Smith lamp lined with silver leaf hangs over the large round table in the corner. Tables are set with long handled forks and spoons for the *aperitivos* and pristine linen dish towels replace the traditional napkins.

Soon after guests are seated, they are presented with the menu. Most choose a personalised tasting menu but nothing is imposed and diners certainly don't have to eat the exact same things as their tablemates. The menus are calibrated so that courses flow evenly and the meal has a balanced rhythm. Juan Mari, Elena or the maitre d' help guide diners in their choices, as the printed menu is more poetic than didactic in nature. At ease in the brightly lit room, Juan Mari stops off at each table to say hello to old friends, engage first-time visitors and express concern that someone hasn't finished her wild boar. "It's a strong flavour if you're not used to game, but it's delicious!" Would she like something else? How about lamb with lotus root?

The *aperitivos*, small bites sent out by the kitchen before the meal, change seasonally and are followed by two or three savoury starters: perhaps mackerel marinated in anise-based *Patxaran* liquor with a dusting of purple corn powder; lobster with fresh bee pollen and pickled vegetables; or spider crab with a touch of lingonberry. Then... there's an egg dish. There is always an egg.

Eggs are Juan Mari's favourite food. They stand in memory of darker days when animal protein wasn't as readily available and a fried egg for supper was a treat. These days, however, eggs at Arzak have nothing to do with the ones you might make at home. A recent egg dish had tomato gummies, *pozole* corn and wild mushrooms. Previous versions have included the colourful Galactic egg with *piquillo* peppers and the iconic egg flower with date chorizo.

Rather than choosing just one main course, Juan Mari suggests ordering two half portions, first fish and then meat. In summer, the fish might be *Grilled sole in sugar cane with carrot and white cacao* or *Monkfish with pecan butter and pumpkin and chickpea hieroglyphics...* Meat courses could include *Roast duck with traces of mastic accompanied by feathery textured potato*, or in winter it could be *Venison with cabbage daisies, lashings of broccolini, walnut miso and sweetened holy basil*.

And then there are desserts and *petit fours*. Chocolate is a constant.

Though the journey is a lively one, the meal is unhurried. The restaurant only has one seating for lunch and one for dinner, which allows the diners to linger for as long as they please.

Juan Mari speaks to the guests at every table in Spanish, French, Basque or the occasional phrase or two in English. His tone is deep and reflective when questioned on the merits of an ingredient, but it shifts to a soothing intimacy as he chats with a distinguished French couple and rises again as he jokes with a table of young chefs.

He tries to shake everyone's hand as they leave after lunch, and these days poses for the occasional selfie with culinary students, international chefs, and gastronomic influencers. Restaurante Arzak has long been a place of pilgrimage and the steady stream of devotees shows no sign of slowing down.

Arzak is also a place of origins. Juan Mari helped define a culinary revolution as one of the founders of the New Basque Cuisine movement. In the 1970s Basque chefs responded to the innovation of their French counterparts by creating their own answer to *Nouvelle Cuisine*.

In April 1976, Juan Mari gave a talk at the first congress of the new *Club de Gourmets* held in Madrid. He spoke off the cuff, and nobody seems to remember what he said exactly, but it impressed Paul Bocuse, the leader of the *Nouvelle Cuisine* movement in France. They hit it off, and Bocuse invited Juan Mari and his friend Pedro Subijana from Restaurante Akelarre to visit him in Lyon. The trip was life changing. Although the Basque chefs were already making market-based cuisine, they were swept up by the camaraderie and concepts of the *Nouvelle Cuisine* movement. After a stop to visit the renowned Troisgros family in Roanne, the two chefs returned home, certain that they could do something similar with Basque Cuisine.

They gathered a few like-minded friends who had restaurants, and the energetic young group spent a year hosting monthly dinners at each chef's respective restaurant. Working together, they tested their creative and original dishes, often comparing a traditional recipe to one of their latest creations. Chefs, friends, a few members of the press, and other gastronomes were invited to taste their latest. A discussion on techniques, ingredients or the merits of a particular dish followed each dinner. It was a lively forum and gave shape to their movement.

They lightened sauces, researched forgotten dishes from the past, and tinkered with new ideas to develop highly original and comparatively delicate recipes, while remaining true to age-old flavours of the Basque region: fish, onion and parsley. The hearty *Chipirones en su tinta* – stewed squid in black ink sauce – became grilled baby squid with ink sauce on the side. Basque standards, such as *Merluza en salsa verde* – hake in green sauce – were codified. Dishes developed by Juan Mari (such as his *Pastel de krabarroka*, a kind of fish terrine that was among his early innovations in 1971) have become staples in Spanish homes. They are endlessly reproduced by home cooks and catering companies, and they're even widely available in supermarkets.

Familiarity is an important factor. The food at Arzak is always connected, however slender the thread may seem, to the classic flavours of Basque cooking. It appeals equally to locals who know the original dishes and destination diners who travel the world for unique tastes.

San Sebastian's food was revered long before there were 'foodies'. Set on the Cantabrian Sea, the city backs up to fertile green mountains filled with wild mushrooms and game, small family farms, and shepherds making artisanal cheeses. It was transformed into a chic summer resort in the mid-19th century when the Spanish royal family began to visit. The aristocracy naturally followed. During the Belle Époque, from the 1880s to the 1920s, San Sebastian attracted grand families from Europe's capital cities who spent their summer season in residence. They would often bring their household chefs from Madrid, Paris or Berlin. The chefs would hire local women as kitchen help year after year. Armed with the knowledge they gained from great continental chefs, these young women used their new skills to refine their traditional dishes back home. Many opened restaurants along the city's river, which large families could reach by boat on day trips out of the city. One such restaurant on the banks of the Urumea river, Fago-llaga, is still run by a great-grandson of one of these women.

In 1897, at the height of the Belle Époque, the young King Alfonso XIII summered in San Sebastian with his mother, the Queen Regent María Cristina. That same year, in the village of Altza, just outside of the city and surrounded by farmland, Juan Mari's paternal grandparents Escolastica and Juan Ramón founded the family business as a simple wine cellar in Arzak-Enea.

Cooking was not a future most parents wanted for their children at that time. Francisca 'Paquita' Arratibel, Juan Mari's mother, was no exception. When her husband, Juan Ramón Arzak, died suddenly in 1951, she was forced to run Arzak on her own out of necessity. The business evolved from a wine cellar into a popular tavern, with Paquita's hearty cooking a big part of its success. Restaurante Arzak became a place to celebrate banquets, christenings and weddings, drawing people to the edges of the city. Young Juan Mari discovered that he enjoyed being behind the bar, making coffee for guests, teasing the waitresses, and joking with the regulars. At the same time, he recognized how tough life was in the kitchen with its long hours, heavy lifting and the intense heat of the coal fires. The image of his mother plucking chickens and moving huge stock pots stayed with him. The following year, at the age of ten, he readily agreed to go off to boarding school in El Escorial, just north of Madrid.

Upon graduation he was headed for a career as a technical architect. To pick up a bit of cash, he was persuaded by a friend to work weekends in restaurants and at catered events in Madrid. The money was quick and it was fun. So much so, that in 1962, he secretly enrolled in the *Escuela Superior de Hostelería y Turismo de Madrid*. Paquita wasn't happy but began to come around during his second year at the school when he cooked her a pheasant stuffed with foie gras and truffles *al estilo Alcantara*. Thereafter she allowed him to man the grill at Arzak when he was home on holiday. From Paquita he learned to take his time, to seek out the best raw ingredients, to peer into the eyes of fish to see if they were at their freshest and to keep purveyors in check with a raised eyebrow. She fostered in her son a respect for the seasons – which also made economic sense – and their traditional cuisine. She taught him her recipes, her techniques, and how to gauge the perfect cooking point of each dish. But Juan Mari insists that the most important lesson she gave him was humility.

In 1966, after spending a few months in London unsuccessfully attempting to learn English, at the age of twenty-four he returned to work in the family restaurant. His mother took a gamble on her son, and little by little he won over a few tables in the dining room. She eventually allowed him to turn a tiny space in the kitchen into a four-table mini restaurant within her own. She must have had a premonition about her son's talent because that same little space is now one of the most coveted chef's tables in the world. At first, nobody came. Quite naturally, locals still preferred his mother's famous roast chicken or garlicky clams in the main dining room. The four sturdy wooden tables covered with long white cloths remained empty most of the time. People simply weren't ready for his experiments on the grill. Still, he persisted on his chosen path. Every year when the restaurant was closed for vacation, he did short *stages* in France, travelling to Paris to visit Alain Senderens and to Frédy Girardet's kitchen in Lausanne, Switzerland.

In 1967, his new wife, Maite Espina, joined the family's restaurant. She updated the décor and took over managing the front of the house. Their first daughter, Marta, arrived in 1968 and Elena came along in 1969.

In the early 70s, recognition and awards began to roll in. By 1974, Juan Mari had earned his first Michelin star and was ushered into the club of the world's top chefs. Although Juan Mari was now a household name at home, Spain was still overlooked on the international culinary scene. After the dictatorship ended with Franco's death in 1975 and Spain became a democracy, the country let down its hair and experienced a burst of creativity and freedom. It was the social equivalent of the Swinging Sixties. Arzak received its second Michelin star in 1977, but it was an uneasy time of political unrest in the Basque Country.

When Spain joined the European Union in 1986, things started to change. The gritty industrial cities of the north, deep in economic crisis after the dictatorship, saw the writing on the wall and started to clean up. Factories began to revamp equipment and modernize production methods. The outlook was good, and an increase in business visitors meant an increase in business lunches. Riding high on a wave of optimism, regular customers were more likely to try new things at the urging of the chef.

Looking back now, the dishes seem classic – *hake in a silky green parsley sauce, deboned squab breast with sage purée* – but they were revolutionary at the time. It was all about procuring great fresh ingredients and treating them carefully with precise technique. Stocks and broths were slow-cooked and triple-strained. Sauces were reduced and used sparingly. Fish was grilled just to perfection, and desserts were turning away from heavy creams and custards.

With San Sebastian just twelve miles from France, Parisians summering on *La Côte Basque* began to drive to Arzak for lunch. The increase in visitors led to more exposure for Juan Mari's unique cuisine and by 1989 Restaurante Arzak had received the highest distinction awarded by the prestigious *Guide Michelin*: a third star.

Seeking to experiment in different areas, Juan Mari began consulting abroad in the 1990s and collaborating with technology companies. The dishes at Arzak incorporated more influences from his travels, and their presentations became fanciful with plates that lit up and domes filled with smoke.

The 1997 inauguration of the Guggenheim Museum in Bilbao brought art collectors and attracted ever more international visitors. The regional Basque government kicked off a campaign to change the world's perception of the area and Juan Mari became an unofficial ambassador, giving dinners in London, New York and Washington, sometimes in collaboration with friends such as chefs Daniel Boulud and Thomas Keller. He also played a role in inviting chefs such as Heston Blumenthal and Michel Bras to *Gastronomika*, San Sebastian's pioneering culinary conference which began in 1998 as *Lo Mejor de la Gastronomia*.

All these initiatives put the Basque Country on the map as an international culinary destination.

Nowadays Juan Mari is less likely to jaunt off to host a dinner in New York or Mexico. He's still in the kitchen almost daily. More importantly, he's in the laboratory, where his well-honed palate and keen culinary sensibility subtly guide the stages of the creative process.

The role of chef has changed dramatically since Juan Mari began cooking, and the food world is radically different. Chefs have taken on the roles of scientists, artists, consultants, and business developers. Juan Mari and other Basque chefs felt that the evolution of their profession deserved a recognized university degree. They lobbied the government for years and found a suitable partner in Mondragón University. Their pet project bore fruit in 2011 when the Basque Culinary Center opened its doors in San Sebastian. Today, Juan Mari continues to serve on its advisory board.

An enormous point of pride is his daughter. Juan Mari beams, "I won the lottery with Elena." His confidence in her and her expanded role in the restaurant gives him the leeway to come in a bit later in the mornings and leave a bit earlier after service (or even take a day off for lunch with his friends). Nevertheless, the restaurant is at the centre of his life. Although the house he shares with his wife is just a stone's throw away, he is often on the phone with Elena as soon as he arrives home.

Juan Mari's house has a tidy herb garden and a well-manicured lawn. Once you get past the friendly welcome from the couple's dogs, Bruno and Mateo, the front door opens directly onto a luminous kitchen. Dog commands are written in English and Basque on the whiteboard near their leashes, but – judging by the effusiveness of the dogs – more training is needed. The tops of shelves and nearly every other surface are covered with Juan Mari's massive collection of toys: cars, action figures, antique trains, and the latest robots from Japan. His playful side is easy to see in the food he creates, and inspiration is everywhere. The house is filled with novels and cookbooks and a diverse art collection ranging from Eduardo Chillida to a Charles Sandison installation curated by his eldest daughter Marta, an art historian and Arzak's artistic consultant.

A few years ago, Juan Mari made the bold decision to close on Sundays, which has now become a family day. His two grandchildren, who live around the corner, can often be found cannonballing into the backyard pool before a family lunch. His world revolves around food and family, with most of his free time spent around a table or exploring markets at home or abroad. Close to home or farther afield, there is always something that intrigues him. "You have to look at the world with the eyes of a cook and the spirit of a child."

In the same way he absorbs flavours, he soaks up chemistry and mechanics, asking scientists, farmers, engineers, and anybody else who crosses his path a lot of questions of about how things work. The Nobel prize-winning chemist Martin Karplus once spent a week training in the kitchen at Arzak with Juan Mari.

A monolithic potato and truffle dish perforated by large circular shapes on the current menu seems to relate directly to discussions with the late sculptor Eduardo Chillida about negative space. Juan Mari is forever taking careful notes in a worn leather notebook at conferences, in kitchens, and on his travels. Later, all this information will be interpreted through his particular filter and may or may not end up on a plate. "If I knew what the future of food was going to be, there'd be no point in our research," he says. "But I'll be working toward it 'til the end of my days."

Arzak has been a training ground for generations of young chefs and Juan Mari relishes the role of mentor. Cooking schools have sent legions of students to him over decades. Some come recommended by another chef for the traditional year-long *stage* which serves as invaluable work experience, and others come to their summer apprenticeship from culinary school. Established professionals may come for a week or even just a day to observe. The door is always open to former staff and apprentices. Though he probably doesn't want to be thought of as every Spanish chef's father and would certainly throw his hands up at 'grandfather', he has, in their regard, become just that.

His eye on the future has never blinked. Even after seventy-some years of changing seasons, he has no interest in resting on his laurels. The waves crashing along San Sebastian's Paseo Nuevo, the bustling street markets in the early morning hours, earthy mushrooms hunted in quiet forests, silvery anchovies straight from the dock, radiant heat from the charcoal grill, the energy of countless kitchen brigades, two culinary revolutions, and a plethora of innovations keep him searching, looking for the next new thing rather than contemplating the past. Sitting in the front row at the cutting-edge *Dialogos de Cocina* conference, he says, "*Hombre*, you can't think of yourself as some sort of guru – there's always something to learn."

«You have to look at the world with the eyes of a cook and the spirit of a child.»

Juan Mari Arzak

3

The
Laboratory

A recipe for creativity

El Laboratorio, the creative centre of Arzak, is a luminous space the size of a small apartment, reached by climbing two narrow flights of stairs and circling through the wine cellar. A reinforced door opens to a large island with a state-of-the-art Samsung induction cooktop and three desks pushed together. The desks are covered with boxes of Turkish *pişmaniye*, USB drives, bags of ancient grains, and jars of seaweed, along with papers, computers and a well-worn copy of Harold McGee's *On Food and Cooking*.

Another door, in this house of doors, is imprinted with a photograph by renowned food photographer Sergio Coimbra. The photograph is of a bright red fractal – a component of one of the restaurant's signature desserts. This door separates the lab's kitchen from a round table where the day's findings are discussed. Lining a wall of the lab, from floor to ceiling, are shelves stacked with small plastic containers holding spices, candies, teas, and other ingredients that serve as a visual catalogue for creativity. Each container bears a scannable QR code, which gives the team access to a database with the classifications and properties of each product.

Xabier Gutierrez presides over the laboratory. He looks every bit the mad scientist in his custom paint-splattered chef's coat, hair sticking out in every direction, and glasses akimbo. Tomorrow's design might feature a silk-screened knife down the back.

Igor Zalakain is a tall matinee idol in chef's whites. Today he's hunched over his computer researching *hoja santa*, a peppery herb he brought back from a recent visit to Mexico City.

Mikel Sorazu, sporting a salt and pepper beard, deliberates over the flavours in a saucepan, tasting and making notes in a black notebook. He's in from London, where he's been training new staff at Ametsa, the Michelin-starred restaurant that the Arzaks oversee at the Halkin Hotel in Belgravia. After a stint at Ametsa, Jon Gutierrez – Xabier's son – has also joined the creative team at Arzak.

Arzak's cuisine is in constant evolution: more than fifty original dishes are created in the laboratory every year, and they're incorporated into menus throughout the seasons. The father-daughter collaboration that has defined the restaurant for over twenty years distinguishes it from its peers. Juan Mari and Elena complement each other flawlessly, and their creativity is seamless. Working with their team like a tight jazz ensemble, they keep a steady beat, listening and riffing in reply as they jam. Their original concepts, their exchanges, their tests and adjustments: each step is further enriched by input from staff and regular patrons in a process that may take months, or even years, of development. By the time a dish reaches the printed menu, no single person can be identified as its creator: at Arzak teamwork reigns supreme. *Siempre es Arzak*. They are all Arzak.

During the development process, a dish's foundation may depend on a specific ingredient or technique that fascinates the team, but something keeps it from coming together. Time marches on, the search continues until a new element arrives, if it ever does. *Squab with guitar shavings* was a year in the making. Juan Mari and Elena spoke to the master guitar-maker Vicente Carrillo, who sent a big box of fragrant shavings. It sat in the lab for ages until someone thought to place a small grill and some wood shavings over the squab. When the wood was burned, the smoke's aroma heightened the flavour of the bird, providing a simple solution to a long-standing puzzle.

An established dish might be disassembled and its elements transformed into parts of other evolving dishes. A chocolate apple that looks like a caramelized onion went from a dessert to a garnish; an idea to revive the *Pastel de krabaroka* for a dish evolved into an *amuse-bouche* wrapped in *kataifi*. Endless and enduring mutual support between the laboratory and the kitchen is the key which has sustained their artistic partnership over so many years.

The space now dedicated to research and experimentation was set aside by Juan Mari in 1999, but the initial groundwork was charted years before.

Xabier is a psychologist-turned-chef with a dark sense of humour. He was taking a chocolate course in the late 80s when he ran into Juan Mari in Paris. At the time Juan Mari was looking to delve more into chocolate and offered Xabier a temporary contract to develop desserts, starting in a corner of the kitchen and later moving into the converted apartment upstairs. From the moment Juan Mari brought Xabier into the fold, the two were kindred spirits.

Over the years, Xabier's role in the restaurant and his work space expanded. The little apartment gradually filled with repurposed equipment from technical laboratories: a hot wire cutter used to make architectural models, an early iteration of a freeze-drying machine, and a small copper still to distil aromas. A tiny room within the apartment became known as the Spice Room because it was filled with spices and other ingredients stored in the ubiquitous plastic containers.

Igor came to Arzak straight out of cooking school in 1993, but then left for France, where he spent three-and-a-half years at Michel Bras, consolidating his range of classic techniques and immersing himself in the Bras family's unique cuisine. He returned to take up his position in the laboratory in 1999. Creative, observant and diplomatic, he is a trusted collaborator to both Juan Mari and Elena.

The next decade was a fertile time for creativity. Spain was in the middle of another culinary revolution, this one spearheaded by the Catalan chef Ferran Adrià at his wildly experimental restaurant elBulli. Juan Mari and Ferran clicked from the beginning. Along with a tight community of Spanish chefs, they travelled around the world attending global conferences and embarking on culinary adventures; they visited each other's kitchens and shared techniques and ideas while maintaining their own distinct identities.

"Every restaurant has its own characteristic spirit and philosophy," says Elena. "*Siempre Arzak* embodies our shared beliefs and aspirations which are rooted in collaborative creativity and innovation. Arzak's culinary identity is Basque, research-based, and contemporary. It's a mouthful, I know, but it's what we do. The laboratory is the core of the restaurant, where we work as a team."

For the Arzak team, inspiration is everywhere: a haunting painting, a kitchen tool, or a dropped ice-cream cone. Sometimes, the origins of a dish may come from the focus on a single ingredient. For example, duck, which can stand up to strong flavours, will send you down a very different path than a delicate Dover sole.

The anatomy of a recipe also includes the aesthetics of presentation: the physical structure, colours, and visual textures that a diner experiences even before tasting that first bite. When necessary, the team will design original tableware and physical supports, such as the heavy salt plates they made for an oyster dish. In order to incorporate moving images into the presentation of a dish, they teamed up with an electronics company to devise transparent plates set atop tablets rendering videos of fire and seascapes.

Juan Mari believes, "working as a team produces the best results. One person alone may have a good idea but eight people will have lots more and in all probability something great will come out of it." Despite their expertise, imaginations, palates, and many years of training, a marvellous new creation may not be feasible for inclusion on the restaurant's menu. Some concepts are just ahead of their time, and others simply too complicated to cook outside of the laboratory in a restaurant-scale setting. Surprisingly, only about twenty per cent of what is produced in the lab debuts in the dining room.

Sometimes dishes are grouped into families with a common thread that evolves over time. For example, Elena has a fascination with traditional cooking techniques from around the world. In countries such as Vietnam and Mexico, leaves are used as a cooking vessel. This method was the catalyst for a series of dishes derived from a study of aromas: the warm fig leaf that evokes summer in the Basque Country, the tobacco-like scent of the lotus leaf, and the intense resin-y smell of the Pandamo leaf steered the team down very different creative routes. According to Xabier, "unlike flavour, aromas are rogue. They invade your senses without your permission." An aroma can inspire an appetite; inciting a desire to taste the flavours it promises. "It smells amazing" is likely to be the first thing you hear from diners before they even pick up a fork.

Juan Mari and Elena have an intrinsic understanding of the Basque palate. While they have catalogued more than 1,600 flavours and aromas in their database, the Basque triumvirate of parsley, olive oil and garlic is discreetly present in many of their dishes. Ginger, not normally used in Basque cooking, makes a subtle appearance in many of Arzak's recipes, enhancing the flavour of other ingredients. The use of herbs and spices is deft. Their achievement is the perfectly balanced dish that shines.

In Basque cuisine, few things are as important as the seasons. Winter brings truffles and *percebes* – the highly prized goose-neck barnacles traditionally harvested in Galicia. White asparagus and fresh anchovies are abundant in May, and every summer albacore tuna swim by on their tropic migration from the central Atlantic. The first wild game appears in November, as do cardoons and artichokes. At Arzak, the treatment of these highly seasonal ingredients is remarkably different from year to year, and dishes are rarely repeated from one season to the next. Last year's tuna belly may be served with what seems to be a burning cinnamon stick and this year's tuna may reference a tamale. The flavours and textures of the star Basque products are imprinted on the minds and palates of Juan Mari, Elena, and the rest of the team, like piano keys under Lang Lang's fingers. The anticipation of each season stirs a storm of ideas, challenges, and debates at the kitchen table and in the lab. Juan Mari's and Elena's notebooks are always filled with new ideas and concepts for the future.

Texture is a weird thing. Basques are mad about soft and gelatinous textures, like delicate fish necks or soft *morcilla* sausage made with lots of slow-cooked onion and leek. Not everyone adores that warm and wiggly sensation, so at Arzak it's offset by something crispy. Oysters are always cooked, however briefly, for the same reason. The food is playful and presents unexpected combinations. Sauces are rich and reductions are smooth as expected in the Basque Country.

Like fashion designers, the creative team is always one season ahead. A recipe may be under development for weeks or months before the star ingredient is at its peak. As a concept develops, sometimes an alternate element with similar characteristics (like a sardine) stands in for the main ingredient so that the team can experiment with textures, seasoning and plating. When 'the star' (the anchovy, for example) is ready for its close up, it takes its rightful place in a nearly finished dish. Subtle tweaks are made, and the recipe, handwritten in pencil and accompanied by helpful drawings by Xabier, is sent down from the lab to the restaurant kitchen for final adjustments. Family and friends of the house will be the first diners to taste it – often at the kitchen table. After critiques and subtle tweaks, the cooks in the kitchen reproduce the dish – say, *Grilled hake chins on a coconut and turmeric spiral with 'pearls' and squid crisps* – and if it gets the thumbs-up, it's served in the dining room to a few select guests, as an addition to their tasting menus.

Juan Mari and Elena keep a close eye on the new dishes to gauge guests' reactions during this final evaluation. The last step in a dish's progress from the laboratory to a menu is the final okay by Juan Mari and Elena. In the end, Juan Mari has to like a new dish better than an existing one before it gets a coveted spot on the *à la carte* menu. He's still the boss.

San Sebastian is a popular seaside resort town. Throughout the summer the city is filled with jazz and classical music fans at *Jazzaldia* and *La Quincena Musical*. Anytime the rest of the country is on holiday, the restaurant is fully booked. In September it is a hub for *Zinemaldia*, the city's international film festival, and in October the food world descends for the *Gastronomika* Congress. Come November, everyone needs a rest, so the restaurant closes for three weeks in late autumn. Some head to warmer climes in Mexico, Brazil, or the Canary Islands, while others prefer European capitals or even a road trip across the United States on motorcycles in search of new inspiration.

The post-holiday period is an especially creative time. The team comes back with new visions sparked by natural landscapes, urban environments or free-wheeling conversations with friends. Markets, of course, are always captivating and usually a chef's favourite place to visit in every town or city. Unusual ingredients, tools, or unique vessels brought back from holiday might spark an idea for a new dish.

Donostia, the Basque name for San Sebastian, is another important ingredient. Its rich history and vibrant traditions are omnipresent on Arzak's menus. There are harvest festivals and yearly events centred around single ingredients: egg and potato *tortilla*-making competitions, *marmitako* tastings during the tuna season, and friendly cook-offs between the private eating clubs. Annual rowing races have their origins in the long-gone whaling tradition. Fermented apple cider is brought by boat down the Urumea river in chestnut casks for a celebratory toast in the early days of winter. On January 20th, the feast day of San Sebastian, the whole town dresses up as chefs and Napoleonic soldiers and marches around the city playing the *Tamborrada* – a series of call and response drum marches – for twenty-four hours straight. At the stroke of midnight, the cooks at Arzak pop open champagne bottles, play the *Tamborrada* and dance the conga through the restaurant. References to all of it may appear on the menu.

Food is an integral part of the Basque identity. The members of the creative core – Juan Mari, Elena, Xabier, and Igor – were born in four different decades, and each brings a unique take on enduring traditions to the small round table in the lab where the future of Arzak is being forged day by day.

«The lab is the core of the restaurant, where we work as a team. We like to describe our cooking as signature, Basque, creative, exploratory and avant-garde cuisine.»

Elena Arzak

The Chef's
Table

The Extended Family

Juan Mari is not a morning person. It's midday when he pops through the back door and goes directly to a chair in front of the pass, where he slips out of his shirt and into a freshly pressed white coat. Marta Mirasolain, his assistant, greets him with her agenda in hand and presents him with the day's schedule, her notes on special reservations, and the requests for interviews, conference appearances, or filming.

Elena has already been in the restaurant for a couple of hours. She has her own pile of requests and notes, which she goes over in the minuscule glass office they share just off the kitchen. The door is usually open, and her eyes don't miss a thing as cooks and *stagiers* set up their *mise en place*.

As soon as the staff meal is cleared *la mesa de la cocina*, the kitchen table, is set for four or more, depending on who's coming for lunch. Elena's mother, Maite Espina, always fashionably dressed and with her hair impeccably styled, is there a few days a week. She has recently retired, but she continues to keep an eye on the accounting that she had handled for so many years. Maite was responsible for the first transformation of Arzak into a fine-dining restaurant. She was able to work the front of the house when her children were young thanks to an aunt who helped with the girls at home. Maite's constant presence made her an integral part of the restaurant's economic stability, which gave her husband – and later her youngest daughter – the freedom to create without worry. The architect Manu Lamosa, Elena's husband, has been instrumental in the most recent physical transformation of Arzak-Enea. He usually stops by to have lunch with his wife, and in the summer their two children might also be at the table for the family meal. Nora, 15, is lively and studious and takes after her mother. Mateo, 11, is a ball of energy and often has a hacked Lego or Transformer by his place setting. He has lately started preparing experiments for his mother and grandfather, who critique them gently but truly.

The remaining seats at the table may be for old friends stopping by for an *aperitivo* and a chat, or for the occasional journalist or visiting chef. One weekend it might be Massimo Bottura, Dominique Crenn, Hélène Darroz or a local colleague like Andoni Luis Aduriz of Mugaritz. On a recent Tuesday, Francis Paniego from Echaurren in La Rioja joined the family for lunch. Paniego had apprenticed at Arzak as a young chef before returning to his family's restaurant, where he earned two Michelin stars.

The long marble chef's table, is, in effect, the control centre where the daily business of the restaurant is orchestrated and played out. The activity around the table includes a parade of visitors who stop by briefly to present their discoveries and suggestions. Itziar Bandrés stops in with some new pottery which might work for a dish they are planning. Xabier comes down from the lab with the results of the morning's experiments: today it might be pickled, fermented or freeze-dried carrot, all part of a progress report on an exercise which is a component of a more involved study, or perhaps some of the new chocolates to see if recent changes in the fillings are to the Arzaks' liking. Everyone has a voice.

Hearing the call of "Who made these potatoes?" a chef from the back hurries to the table to explain the process in detail, but one bite tells Juan Mari that something is not right. He swiftly corrects it.

Igor descends from his station in the laboratory with a proposal for Elena's next presentation at Madrid Fusion, the annual culinary summit. Both Arzaks have been travelling to and speaking at conferences internationally for years, promoting Basque gastronomy and fostering connections and communication between chefs. Like everything else, the genesis of many of those talks happens at the kitchen table. This book started there, too.

Mariano, the sommelier, holds court with winemakers and distributors before the lunch service. Occasionally he appears at the kitchen table for a consultation with a particularly choice bottle in one hand and the proper stemware in the other. Mariano has been with Arzak for thirty-eight years and manages a 100,000-bottle cellar. More than 70 percent of the wines are Spanish, 20 percent French and the rest are from all over the world. Though Arzak's cellar shows its reverence for the acknowledged best of Spain and France with no shortage of grand names from Rioja and Burgundy, there are a lot of unexpected small producers and local wines like the crisp Basque white Txakoli, as well as rare bottles from around the world. It's a well-curated cellar. The collection was built over many generations of the Arzak family and continues to grow.

For years the wine was stored in smaller cellars throughout the building, and some was even kept in Juan Mari's house; in those days, if a diner ordered a rare bottle, the sommelier would send someone on a motorbike. Today, the newly designed wine cellar means that Mariano finally has the entire collection in one place.

The modern bodega is an engineering marvel. It is located on an upper story of the ancient house and circles an old support beam made from a single tree trunk that is still the symbolic heart of the building. Humidity and temperature are rigorously controlled. Tiny fibre optic lights help keep these elements in balance during the lunch and dinner services, when sommeliers and servers are searching for and fetching bottles.

The action at the kitchen table is steady as packages of new ingredients, gifts, and foodstuffs arrive. A birthday cake for Mari Jose, one of the waitresses, is cut. María from the administration department comes down from her office with a payroll question. A neighbour brings a half dozen eggs from her chickens just for Juan Mari, while another raps on the window with some aloe vera she's just trimmed from a massive plant behind the restaurant – do they want it? Surely the boys in the lab can do something with it. She's not taking no for an answer, so Igor graciously accepts the gift and takes it away. A shepherd brings a wheel of cheese for Elena because he knows she's crazy about it. A Swiss couple on their way to the western province of Asturias drops by to say hello: their daughter knew Elena at hospitality school. They stay and chat over a glass of wine and a parade of the latest *aperitivos*.

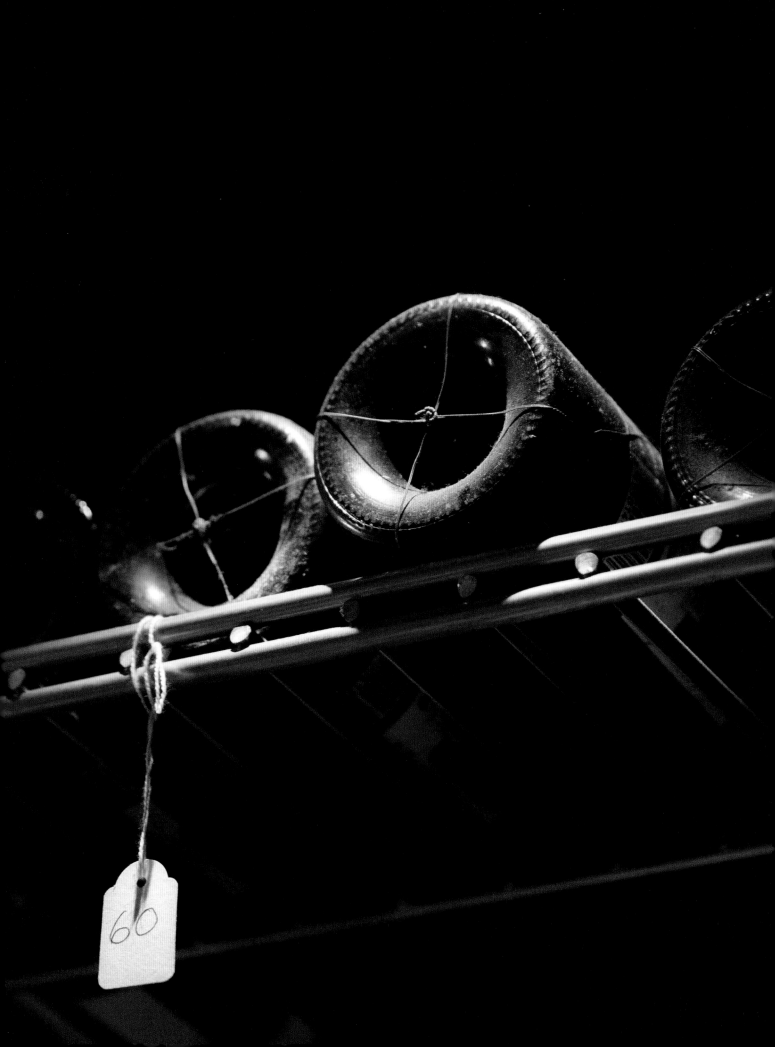

A few years ago, on a hot summer day during the annual *Vuelta de España* bike race, crowds – including a few chefs and guests – gathered in front of the restaurant in the midday sun to watch the cyclists pass. At one point a flustered young mother with a new-born baby came into the restaurant, upset because all the buses had been rerouted and she could not get home. Just as any good neighbour would do, Elena set her up at the kitchen table and cooed at the baby. The Arzaks are part of the fabric of their city.

As soon as service begins, the steady stream of visitors shifts from the table to the pass. Chefs, wine-makers, and diners from around the world or from down the street want to see the kitchen in action before being shown to their tables in the dining room. Juan Mari and Elena both have an amazing capacity for re-membering names, faces and details.

The sought-after and celebrated chef's table is unsurprisingly the most requested seat in the house for dining. Reservations are booked months in advance. Each day, the transition from command centre to chef's table is ra-pid. The Arzaks and any other visitors scatter – to the dining room, lab, offi-ce or bar. The table is dressed and laid by waitresses who advance with hea-vy, ironed tablecloths and silver place settings. A sleek multi-coloured light fixture designed by Borja Azkarate, who oversaw the renovation of the di-ning rooms, hangs over the table.

Service at Arzak has a formal air but is never stiff, and the group at the chef's table is immediately put at ease by the welcoming staff. The congenial spi-rit of the Arzak kitchen flows into the main dining rooms and toward the chef's table. It is a convivium which re-flects the Basques' love of preparing a meal to be shared. However, a seat at the chef's table is never guaran-teed. Sometimes the marble surface is needed for a specific preparation, in which case it is quickly colonized by young cooks who set about working chocolate, caramel or another pro-cess that requires a cool surface.

Saturdays at the kitchen table are for family. Juan Mari's elder daughter, Marta, makes it home to San Sebas-tian every weekend to take her place at the table. Guests and interruptions are discouraged, and although eating in a kitchen with thirty busy cooks and a looming lunch reservation for that very table may not seem like anyone's idea of intimate, it is a sacred hour for the Arzaks.

Family is the most important in-gredient for Basques. The Arzaks, gathered in their old house and su-rrounded by staff and visitors, are no exception.

The facility is an engineering prodigy located in an upper floor of the old house, surrounding an ancient tree log that is still the symbolic heart of the building.

The Kitchen

Elena Arzak and the future

The Arzak family have managed the transition from father to daughter gradually, over the course of a decade. When pressed about the succession of his daughter, Juan Mari responds in Basque, "*Orain oraingo eta gero geroko.*" Now the present and later the future.

That future is imminent.

Looking toward it, the façade of the 120-year-old building recently got a face lift, its sturdy bones clad in a striking new zinc coat. But the big questions on the lips of critics and contemporaries are: What's happening in the kitchen? Where is Arzak headed in its second century?

Elena Arzak is the person who will make that decision. Just shy of fifty, Elena exudes confidence as she ties a long white apron tightly around her slim waist and tucks a pen into the side pocket of her tailored chef's jacket. She surveys the kitchen: this is her turf. Cooking is her chosen profession. Raised in the restaurant, she fell in love with this kitchen as a young girl. The smell of seafood boiling and the rhythmic backbeat of orders being read through the intercom takes her back to a childhood of assigned tasks and routines, cleaning squid, peeling oranges, and rolling chocolate truffles at the marble table in front of the pass. She would have happily spent all of her days in the kitchen, but her parents stressed the importance of a formal education and they wanted both Elena and her sister to have options outside the family business.

Like many young chefs, at age eighteen Elena set out to see the culinary world. She studied at the esteemed Schweizerische Hotelfachschule Luzern in Switzerland, followed by apprenticeships in some of the world's great restaurants: La Gavroche in London; the Troisgros family restaurant in Roanne; a year at Carré des Feuillants and Le Vivarois in Paris. To refine her training, she did shorter stints at Alain Ducasse's Louis XV de Montecarlo, at elBulli in Roses on the Costa Brava with Ferran and Albert Adrià, and with the iconoclastic French chef Pierre Gagnaire at his eponymous restaurant in Paris. When her training felt solid, she faced the inevitable challenge – going home to the family restaurant, where her father was also one of the most influential chefs in Europe.

While working her way through all of the stations of Restaurante Arzak's kitchen – from fish to vegetables to desserts – Elena strove to maintain her independence, developing her own ideas and flavour palate. "My father has always motivated people and he motivated me as he would any of the young chefs," she says. "He always believed in the members of his team, so right from the beginning I was creating dishes. I was nineteen when I made my first original dish for him."

Juan Mari's insistence that Elena constantly create new dishes, which they would critique together, defined her style. Her mornings in the back of the kitchen were dedicated to this exercise. She started by reducing the number of elements in each recipe to place a focus on the star ingredient, cutting down on sugar in the desserts, and playing with colour to alter the diner's taste sensations, and by midday she presented the finished dishes to her father. This led to a fruitful, collaborative relationship and they continue to challenge each other to this day.

As she promoted her own ideas, Elena kept her ego in check, ensuring the development of habits that sharpen the critical skills of attention and reflection that allow learning. Unlike her father, who is something of an anarchist in the kitchen, Elena's approach is systematic, whether in the development of a single recipe or the flow of an entire menu. Where Juan Mari may challenge established order directly, even disruptively, Elena tends to proceed by analysis, admitting a preference for control. No matter how they go about their work, they share a common palate deeply rooted in Basque flavours and, of course, their DNA. They know instinctively what works for Arzak and that's the secret to their success.

For as long as Elena could remember, her father had been famous and the restaurant was always filled with renowned and distinguished guests alongside local families. But back then, the world's fascination with chefs and food was in its infancy. When Elena first sat at the kitchen table as a girl, chefs still spent most of their time in the kitchen. Today, from that same table, she oversees a full-time staff of fifty. As she watches Cyntia Yaber, the *chef de cuisine*, carefully weighing truffles and measuring the exact length of a piece of potato with a metal ruler, Elena explains the inspiration and techniques behind some of the restaurant's dishes for a group of Korean chefs sitting down for lunch. Later she curates dinner for the American arbiter of food, Anthony Bourdain, who is in deep conversation with her father as cameras filming an episode of his television show *Parts Unknown* hover everywhere.

Elena is in the kitchen early. She prefers to go over her correspondence with her assistant, Monica Rico, while the restaurant is still relatively quiet. Honoured in 2012 as World's Best Female Chef by the World's 50 Best Restaurants list, she has had an avalanche of requests to speak at conferences, give interviews, and cook private dinners abroad. She gently declines most with a thoughtful personal note. Never complacent as the weight of running the restaurant now passes to her, she steers it with a firm hand. She speaks in a low, stern tone when correcting a staff member, but she's not above raising it should the occasion warrant. Elena tastes her way through the kitchen, pausing to deliberate with the head of a section over the desired degree of crispness for one of the snacks or showing a young cook how to extract tiny chocolate frogs from their moulds without damaging the complicated shapes. She tweaks the plating of a dish on the pass, edits recipes, and reviews anything that is going out of the restaurant with her name on it. The staff is on familiar terms with Elena, yet they treat her with respect, in the same way they've always done with her father.

Some would call the Arzaks alchemists, but Elena considers herself and her father to be artisans. She fully subscribes to their philosophy of constant innovation and evolution, of adapting to changing times and the way people like to eat. But no matter where the search for new ways to interpret the world around her leads, home and family remain her touchstones.

Arzak is research-based. While Elena is close to the land and to the people who produce the raw ingredients for their kitchen, Arzak doesn't have a garden or raise its own chickens. The waters, hills and fields of the Basque Country are the restaurant's farms and gardens. Elena continues to nurture strong relationships with suppliers and can often be found on any given Tuesday morning at San Sebastian's central market, La Bretxa, talking to Mari Carmen, a spry farm lady in her mid-80s, about what to do with the tops of onions or sizing up bonito with Fernando, her fishmonger. Like her father, she is also on a mission to recover the pleasure of flavour while maintaining a contemporary sensibility. Apart from the constant innovation for which Arzak has always been known, one of the things that sets the restaurant apart is the depth of knowledge that she and her father have accumulated over the family's long history. She doesn't want to lose any of that legacy as she strives to find ways to incorporate the richness of traditional Basque flavours into the dishes of the future. "My biggest challenge," she says, "is anticipating people's changing tastes and staying one step ahead."

All of the principals live near the restaurant and Elena is no exception. Her brick apartment building sits on a leafy street down the hill from the restaurant. She shares a three-bedroom apartment with her husband, Manu, and their two children. The living room feels lived in, with books, toys and computer games strewn around. The open, American-style kitchen is next to the living room. Spanish kitchens were traditionally closed off behind a door to keep cooking odours, especially fish, from spreading throughout the house. But Elena, who cooks a lot of fish at home, doesn't want to spend her home time behind a door and away from her family. She has cooked with her children at home since they were old enough to stand on a chair by the stove. She sees it as an important part of anyone's education, instilling in them the nutritional and social importance of this skill. "What if friends show up on your doorstep unexpectedly? You've got to be able to improvise!" she reminds them. Every Saturday, her children have their meals at the restaurant's kitchen table with their parents, grandparents and aunt and in the dining room on special occasions.

Education is a priority in the Arzak family. Elena was educated at the German International school in San Sebastian, considered one of the city's best. In addition to her native Spanish, she also speaks German, English, French and Basque. As she's travelled the world, her proficiency in languages has stood her in good stead. She would like her children to have the same advantage. Both attend school in San Sebastian. Nora is a good student, but she finds time to also play football and play the piano. Mateo is currently applying his energies to his love of airplanes as well as his own language studies in French and English. He is very creative. Elena wants them to choose their own futures. The restaurant will always be there if they chose that path.

The world is changing. Gastronomy is changing. The way we communicate is changing. Elena knows her role as a chef has also changed. She is deeply human. Awareness and social responsibility are important to her. Recently she made the decision to rethink many things at the restaurant, from how to share ideas across cultures to how the restaurant can work with producers to be more sustainable and even how she can make the staff happier. In addition to leading her team, she feels a responsibility as a representative of her country and her culture to be part of the change.

"We can't just continue to polish and refine what we are doing now," she says. "We need to think about tomorrow and make sure that shine is sustainable. Everyone is in such a hurry these days. At Arzak we don't subscribe to that. We are a 120-year-old restaurant. I'm the fourth generation of my family to be behind the stove. I have shared this kitchen with my father for a long time now and someday I'll carry the baton by myself. It's wonderful but very complicated. I don't feel the need to revolutionize the whole restaurant. Our culinary tendencies don't change from one day to the next, nor from year to year. The continual work we do on them simply helps us to discover new paths. I've grown up watching pots cook over a low flame and plans take shape just as slowly at the kitchen table. That's the life I want for my family, my team, my nation and I will defend it, wooden spoon in hand."

«My biggest challenge is foreseeing the unpredictable tastes of people and staying ahead of them.»

Elena Arzak

6

64
Recipes

Recipe Index

HAKE WITH
CHICKPEA PAINT

120

RED MULLET
WITH OAK LEAVES

122

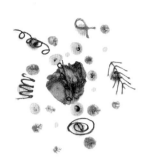

SYMBOLIC SQUAB

124

STRATA AND HAKE
KOKOTXAS

128

WHITE TUNA
AND QUINOA

130

CRISPY CREPE
LOBSTER

132

BLACK
LEMONS

136

WHITE TUNA
TAMALE

138

TERPENE
SQUAB

140

SEA BREAM
WITH NASTURTIUM LEAVES

144

SEABERRY
MILK POT

146

LICENCE TO KRILL

148

RADIANT
ANTHOCYANIN DUCK

152

BAMBOO AND
KOKOTXAS

154

HAZELNUT PARFAIT
WITH DRIED STRAWBERRIES

156

VEAL STEW
WITH 'INK'

160

PISTACHIO STONE
AND CITRUSY BEETROOT

162

ON A RAZOR'S EDGE

164

EMPANADILLAS

168

ANISE AND APPLE
ROSQUILLAS

170

'CORN ON THE COB'
WITH TRUFFLES

172

ANOTHER BRICK IN THE
CHOCOLATE AND MUSTARD WALL

176

WHITE TUNA
AND RHUBARB

178

KUMQUATS WITH
CAMU CAMU

180

DUCK AND
GUITAR SHAVINGS

184

GIANT CHOCOLATE
TRUFFLE

186

BABY SQUID WITH
BLACK TOMATO

188

EGGETARIAN

192

SQUID ON
LEAVES

194

EAT YOUR FRUIT
AND VEG

196

RED CHILLI PEPPER
VENISON

200

CHOCOLATE AND
COLOURED SHARDS

202

LOBSTER
CORALINE

204

BLOOD-RED
APPLE

208

DUCK
AND BIRDSEED

210

REEF(ER) LOBSTER
WITH HEMP SEED MUSTARD

212

SOLE IN CANE

216

SOY DUCK

218

OYSTERS
MONDRIAN

220

LOBSTER AND
BEE POLLEN

224

WHITE TUNA
WITH GARLIC PETALS

226

SQUAB WITH
POTATO FEATHERS

228

SPACE EGG

232

CHARCOAL-GRILLED
OYSTERS

234

HIBISCUS ICE CREAM
AND BEETROOT CRUMBLE

236

NECTARINE AND
SQUID VINES

240

ORANGE DUCK

242

CHOCOLATE
ONION

244

GREEN TEA AND ONION
CROMLECH
126

PINEWOOD
SQUAB
134

LADYBIRD
LADYBIRD
142

PRAWNS AND CHARRED LEMONS
WITH PATCHOULI
150

FISH OUT
OF WATER
158

FLAMING
CHICKPEA STEW
166

MONKFISH
AT LOW TIDE
174

CHOCOLATE
FOREST
182

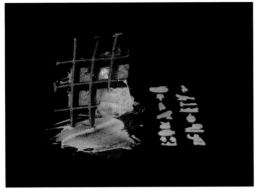

MONKFISH
CLEOPATRA

190

SIZZLING SQUID

198

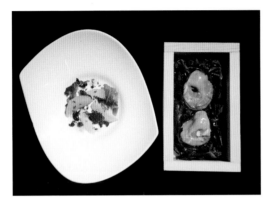

OYSTERS WITH
HAM AND CITRUS

206

WHITE TUNA
AND CINNAMON

214

STOMPED
FRUIT

222

THE KOBE'S
BEER

230

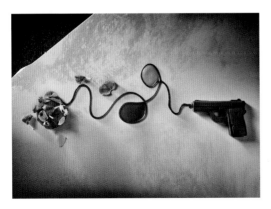

A SHOT OF
CHOCOLATE

238

HONEYMEAD AND
FRACTAL FLUID

246

HAKE WITH CHICKPEA PAINT

— Serves 4. —

MOJO SAUCE

50 g desalted cod
50 g toasted bread
50 g olive oil (0.4%)
50 g sherry vinegar
50 g milk
Salt and pepper

HAKE

4 hake loins (125 g each)
Salt

YELLOW PAINT

30 g roasted almond praline
*250 g cooked chickpeas (cooked slowly
with onion and carrot)*
7 g lemon juice
1.5 g turmeric
Salt and pepper

GREEN PAINT

1.5 g guarana seed powder
3 g ground caraway seeds
300 g green sauce*
15 g chive juice
Salt and pepper
Ginger powder

RED PICKLES

8 pickled baby gherkins
125 g water
0.5 g cochineal food colouring
1.8 g kappa carrageenan
0.25 g powdered red food colouring

BLACK CAPER BERRIES

8 pickled caper berries (with stem)
2 sachets squid ink
125 g water
1.8 g kappa carrageenan

YELLOW CAULIFLOWER

150 g cauliflower
125 g water
1.8 g kappa carrageenan
1 g turmeric

*GREEN SAUCE

1 garlic clove, finely chopped
½ tbsp parsley, finely chopped
3 tbsp olive oil (0.4%)
5 g wheat flour
50 g clams
300 g cold water
Salt

MOJO / Mix all the ingredients in a food processor and pulverize until smooth. Adjust salt and pepper if necessary. **HAKE** / Coat the hake with the mojo sauce and cook on a hot flat top grill or frying pan. Remove before fully cooked and set aside. **YELLOW PAINT** / Mix all the ingredients and bring to a boil. Pulverize until smooth and season with salt and pepper. **GREEN PAINT** / Boil the green sauce with the guarana and caraway seeds. Pulverize until smooth, adding the chive juice at the last minute. Season with salt, pepper and ginger. **RED PICKLES** / Combine all the ingredients except the gherkins in a food processor and pulverize. Put in a saucepan and bring to a boil. Skewer the gherkins with a needle and dip them into the red mixture. Set aside. **BLACK CAPER BERRIES** / Combine all the ingredients except the capers in a food processor and pulverize. Put in a saucepan and bring to a boil. Hold the capers by the stem and dip them into the black mixture. Set aside. **YELLOW CAULIFLOWER** / Break the cauliflower into eight pieces and cook lightly in salted boiling water. Drain and cool. Combine the rest of the ingredients in a food processor, pulverize and bring to a boil. Skewer the cauliflower pieces with a needle and dip them into the yellow mixture. Set aside. **GREEN SAUCE** / Put the oil, garlic, and half of the chopped parsley in a saucepan over medium-high heat. Before the garlic begins to brown, add the flour and sauté for a few minutes. Add the clams. Add the water and cook for about 3 minutes. Add the remaining parsley. Remove the clams and save them for another recipe. Set sauce aside.

PLATING / Plate the fish over wide brush strokes of the green and yellow paint. Garnish with red pickles, black capers and yellow cauliflower.

RED MULLET
WITH OAK LEAVES

— Serves 4. —

RED MULLET

2 red mullets
Olive oil
Salt and pepper

LOBSTER OIL EMULSION

2 lobster heads
300 g extra virgin olive oil
1 egg
Juice of ¼ lemon
Salt and pepper

COURGETTE AND RED PEPPER LEAVES

½ medium courgette
½ red pepper
Olive oil for frying
Salt and pepper

POTATO AND BEETROOT LEAVES

1 potato
150 g beetroot juice
Olive oil for frying
Salt and pepper

ANISE AND DILL LEAVES

100 g extra virgin olive oil
1 tsp anise seed
1 tsp dried dill
2 sheets phyllo dough

STRAWBERRIES WITH ANISE

4 strawberries
A drop of anise leaf essential oil

CASSAVA TUBE

Piece of cassava
1 garlic clove
200 g olive oil
Pinch of thyme
Salt

OTHER INGREDIENTS

4 mint or nettle leaves

RED MULLET / Fillet and debone the red mullet. Save the tails and backbone. Season the fillets and fry them in a little olive oil. Set aside. Fry the tails and bones in hot oil. Drain and season. **LOBSTER OIL EMULSION** / Halve the lobster heads. Cook them in oil at 120ºC for 2 hours. Allow to cool. Beat the egg with a pinch of salt and the lobster oil until it creates a firm emulsion. Add the lemon juice. Adjust the salt and pepper. **COURGETTE AND RED PEPPER LEAVES** / Peel both vegetables and cut into thin horizontal slices. Cut into leaves using an oak leaf shaped cookie cutter. Dry in a dehydrator and fry in oil at a low temperature without burning. Season with salt and pepper. **POTATO AND BEETROOT LEAVES** / Peel and cut the potato into thin slices. Cut into leaves using an oak leaf shaped cookie cutter. Soak for 20 minutes in beetroot juice. Drain, spread out and dry in a dehydrator. Fry in oil over low heat, taking care not to burn. Season with salt and pepper. **ANISE AND DILL LEAVES** / Mix half of the olive oil with the anise and the other half with the dill. Pulverize separately and let settle. Use an oak leaf or similar shaped cookie cutter to cut the phyllo dough. Paint half of the leaves with the anise oil and the rest with the dill oil. Dehydrate until crisp. Fry over low heat and repaint with the respective oils. Season with salt and pepper. **STRAWBERRIES WITH ANISE** / Cut the strawberries in half and dress them with the same oil used for the anise leaves. **CASSAVA TUBE** / Cut the cassava into 5 cm thick tubes. Confit in the oil along with the garlic and thyme. Drain and season.

PLATING / Plate the red mullet fillet surrounded by the different crunchy leaves, mint, and lobster oil emulsion. Garnish with the strawberries, cassava, fried fish bones, and tails.

SYMBOLIC SQUAB

— Serves 4. —

RED MOJO SAUCE

50 g almond praline
1 small roasted tomato
2 strawberries
40 g kimchi sauce
3 roasted red peppers, skinned and seeded
10 g lime juice
75 g olive oil
Salt, pepper and a pinch of sugar

SQUAB SAUCE

2 squab carcasses
3 medium onions
½ head garlic
1 pinch fresh thyme
200 g olive oil
Salt and pepper

SQUAB

2 squabs
Salt, ginger and liquorice powder

SYMBOLS (SEE PHOTO FOR THE SYMBOLS STENCIL)

250 g red cabbage, sliced
1000 g water
150 g rice
100 g purple potato, cooked
20 g parsnips, cooked
Salt and pepper

ORANGE CREAM

190 g orange juice
20 g sugar
9 g kappa carrageenan
A small piece of vanilla bean

BEETROOT AND APPLE BALLS

½ apple
1 beetroot
100 g olive oil (0.4%)
Salt

GREEN OIL

20 g of the squab sauce
6 tbsp oil from the squab sauce
Pinch of parsley powder

OTHER INGREDIENTS

Chopped candied walnuts

RED MOJO SAUCE / Combine all the ingredients and grind into a thick paste in a food processor. Add pepper. Set aside. **SQUAB** / Remove the breasts and season lightly. Coat well with the mojo sauce and cook them on the flat top grill. Set aside. Use the rest of the squab carcass for the sauce. **SQUAB SAUCE** / Clean and chop the vegetables. Sauté in oil until lightly browned. Chop the carcasses and combine them with the vegetables and the thyme and cook until golden. Once everything is fully cooked, strain off the excess oil and set aside. Cover with water and let cook for 90 minutes. Strain and season. At the last minute, add a few drops of the oil used for sautéing. **SYMBOLS** / Boil water and add the red cabbage. Cook for 8 minutes. Remove the cabbage and keep for other recipes. Add the rice and cook for 25 minutes, stirring occasionally. Strain and set the rice aside. Pulverize the potato, parsnip and 150 g of the cooked rice. Season and spoon the purée into a piping bag with a fine nozzle. Make the symbols on a sheet of paper. Dry at 50ºC. Store in the dehydrator until ready to use. **ORANGE CREAM** / Pulverize the ingredients in a professional blender until smooth. Boil the mixture and spread it on a sheet pan. Once it is set and cool, blend again to smooth out the cream. **BEETROOT AND APPLE BALLS** / Using a melon baller, make 8 apple balls and 12 beetroot balls. Boil the beetroot balls in salted water until tender. **GREEN OIL** / Cover the balls with olive oil until they are ready to be used. Mix ingredients without emulsifying.

PLATING / Plate the filleted squab breasts one on top of the other on a bit of red mojo sauce. Put five dots of the orange cream around the squab and place apple balls on top of two of them and beetroot balls on the rest. Lay a different symbol on top of each ball. Decorate the plate with a few dots of orange cream, red mojo and green oil.

GREEN TEA AND ONION CROMLECH

— Serves 4. —

KÉFIR AND FOIE MIXTURE

200 g fresh foie gras
55 g cream cheese
45 g kéfir
1 tbsp extra virgin olive oil
Salt and black pepper, powdered ginger
and powdered liquorice

RED WINE JAM

750 g onion
50 g butter
3 tbsp olive oil
115 g sugar
750 g red wine
150 g white wine vinegar
50 g sherry vinegar
Salt

CROMLECH

200 g cassava flour
150 g turmeric broth (yellow colouring)
150 g huitlacoche broth (black colouring)
Olive oil for frying

GREEN TEA PREPARATION

250 g water
2.5 g matcha green tea
10 g sugar
2.5 g gellan gum

NEPTUNE POWDER

10 g lichen
3 g freeze-dried sea urchin
3 g dried shrimp

CHICKEN POWDER

250 g chicken broth
50 g bread crumbs

OTHER INGREDIENTS

Powdered parsley

KÉFIR AND FOIE / Cut the foie gras into cubes and sauté. Allow to sit for 5 minutes and blend together with the cream cheese, kéfir and olive oil. Season with salt, pepper, and powdered ginger and liquorice. Set aside. **RED WINE JAM** / Clean and julienne the onion. Cook over low heat with the butter, oil and sugar. Do not brown. Once it is soft, add the red wine and the vinegars. Cook the mixture over low heat for 2 hours or until it has a jam-like consistency. Set aside. **CROMLECH** / Mix half the cassava flour with the turmeric broth. Knead the mixture for 5 minutes. Allow to sit for 10 minutes. Repeat with the rest of the cassava flour and the huitlacoche broth. Once both doughs have rested, gently press 2 g of each colour together to make a ball without mixing the colours. Roll out the dough balls between 2 sheets of oven paper until very thin. Fry the sheets of dough at 220°C while stirring the oil in a circular motion for 40 seconds. Then let them sit in olive oil at 149°C for 2 minutes. Drain well and season with salt and pepper. **GREEN TEA** / Heat the water and infuse it with the matcha tea. Add the gellan gum and sugar and bring to a boil. Pulverize in a food processor. **NEPTUNE POWDER** / Grind all the ingredients together until you get a powdery texture. **CHICKEN POWDER** /Pour the hot broth over the bread crumbs and let it absorb completely. Let the crumbs dry at 60°C for 6 hours. Grind into a fine powder.

PLATING / Place part of the foie mixture on a baking sheet. Spread the wine jam thinly on top and repeat with another layer of foie. Quickly coat with the matcha tea and allow it to gel for 20 minutes. Cut into 3 x 3 cm cubes. Make a small cut in the bottom of each cromlech and fill with the kéfir and foie mixture. Stand the filled cromlechs on a plate. Sprinkle with a bit of Neptune, parsley and chicken powders.

Playing with cassava semolina brought us the nice surprise of creating colourful bloated figures, which are very versatile, crispy and, of course, tasty.

—— *Green tea and onion cromlech* ——

STRATA AND HAKE KOKOTXAS

— Serves 4. —

COD MOJO SAUCE

50 g dried salt cod
100 g olive oil
50 g milk
1 roasted spring onion
1 tbsp sherry vinegar
3 drops orange-blossom water
Pinch of codium powder
Pinch of spirulina
Salt and pepper

KOKOTXAS

12 hake kokotxas
Salt

SOUR SAUCE

10 g sherry vinegar
¼ lemon, cubed (remove peel and seeds)
100 g extra virgin olive oil
2 freeze-dried raspberries, lightly crushed
3 mint leaves, finely chopped
Salt and pepper

POTATO CUBES

1 medium potato
125 g extra virgin olive oil
125 g duck fat
4 tbsp cod pil pil sauce
Pinch of thyme
Pinch of rosemary
Pinch of psyllium
Pinch of dried orange peel powder
Salt and sugar

STRATA

2 sheets, 8 x 3 cm, all-butter puff pastry
25 g confectioner's sugar
75 g spirulina powder
Salt and pepper

OTHER INGREDIENTS

A pinch of codium powder and huitla-coche

COD MOJO SAUCE / Pulverize all the ingredients in a food processor except the vinegar and orange-blossom water. Adjust the salt and pepper. Add vinegar and orange-water blossom to taste. Set aside. KOKOTXAS / Clean the kokotxas well and season with salt and pepper. Just before serving, cook them quickly on both sides with a little oil on a flat top grill or frying pan. Sprinkle each one with orange powder. SOUR SAUCE / Thoroughly mix the ingredients. Set aside. POTATO CUBES / Cut the potato into 4 cubes and hollow out the centres. Confit in olive oil and duck fat along with a pinch of rosemary, psyllium and thyme. Once cooked, drain and season lightly. Fill the potatoes with the pil pil sauce and sprinkle with a pinch of psyllium and orange peel powder. STRATA / Bake the puff pastry at 190ºC for 30 minutes. Remove from the oven and cut the puff pastry into 4 rectangles. Continue baking for 8 minutes. Remove from oven and let cool. Salt and pepper the puff pastry and sprinkle with sugar and spirulina.

PLATING / Plate the kokotxas accompanied by the potato cube and the strata. Sauce and finish by dusting with the powdered orange peel, spirulina, codium powder and huitlacoche.

WHITE TUNA
AND QUINOA

— Serves 4. —

WHITE TUNA BELLY

180 g white tuna
125 g kosher salt
Olive oil (0.4%)

QUINOA AND SWEET PAPRIKA OIL

100 g olive oil
10 g sweet paprika
10 g red quinoa

QUINOA OIL

80 g grapeseed oil
15 g red quinoa

QUINOA EMULSION

1 egg
50 g olive oil (0.4%)
1 tbsp turmeric
15 g quinoa, roasted
Salt and pepper

CRISPY QUINOA

110 g water
120 g flour
30 g Trisol (soluble fibre derived from wheat)
25 g red quinoa
Olive oil for frying

OTHER INGREDIENTS

Syrha leaves

WHITE TUNA BELLY / Cut the tuna belly into 1.5 cm slices and pack them in coarse salt for 8 minutes. Remove the salt, clean the fish well and cut into cubes. Cover with olive oil until they are ready to be used. **QUINOA AND SWEET PAPRIKA OIL** / Combine the ingredients and cook at 55ºC for 5 minutes. The oil is ready to use once the mixture settles. **QUINOA OIL** / Pulverize the ingredients in a food processor. Allow the oil to settle. Set aside. **QUINOA EMULSION** / Emulsify the egg with the oil as if it were a mayonnaise. Once it is well emulsified, add the rest of the ingredients. Season with salt and pepper. **CRISPY QUINOA** / Mix all the ingredients in a bowl except the quinoa. Cut some rectangular sheets of oven paper. Spread a thin layer of the flour, turmeric, Trisol and water mixture on each sheet. Sprinkle quinoa on top. Heat the oil to 190ºC and fry until lightly coloured. Drain well and remove the paper.

PLATING / Place the cubes of white tuna on the plate and beside it, the emulsion and the Syrha leaves drizzled with quinoa oil. Add the quinoa and paprika oil and arrange the crispy quinoa for the finishing touch.

CRISPY CREPE LOBSTER

— Serves 4. —

LOBSTER

2 lobsters (350 g each)
Salt
Ginger powder
Liquorice powder

PINEAPPLE MOJO SAUCE

75 g pineapple juice
75 g water
40 g roasted peanuts
Salt and pepper

CRISPY CREPE

280 g water
2 g turmeric
120 g flour
15 g parsley
Olive oil for frying
Salt

TOMATO WATER

2 tomatoes
0.2 g Xantana
Salt and pepper

FRESH LEAVES AND COURGETTE FLOWERS

2 g acai powder
1 tsp olive oil
1 courgette flower
8 JamPet leaves

OTHER INGREDIENTS

green sesame seeds (wasabi flavour)
and red sesame seeds (soy flavour)

LOBSTER / Cut the lobsters in half, separating the tail and the claws from the heads. Set the heads aside for other uses. Thread two wooden skewers through the tails to keep them straight when blanched. Blanche the tails in boiling water and plunge into iced water. Remove the shell. Season with salt and sprinkle with liquorice and ginger powder. Set aside. **PINEAPPLE MOJO SAUCE** / Pulverize all the ingredients until smooth. Season with salt and pepper. **CRISPY CREPE** / Boil 130 g of water with the turmeric. Remove from heat and allow to infuse for 2 minutes. Strain and cool. Mix the turmeric infusion with half of the flour. Set aside. Boil parsley in water for 2 minutes. Drain and cool. Pulverize with 150 g of water in a food processor until smooth. Strain. Mix 120 g of the parsley preparation in a bowl with the rest of the flour. Put a spoonful of each of the batters, one on top of the other, in a warm non-stick frying pan. Once a circle of the two colours has formed, make a few swipes outward to give it a star shape. Let it cook over low heat and remove. Dry at 55ºC and fry in oil at 190ºC so the star puffs up a bit. Season with salt and pepper. **TOMATO WATER** / Pulverize the tomatoes and strain it through a cheese-cloth. Keep the tomato pulp in the cheesecloth. For every 100 g of tomato water add 0.2 g Xantana. Pulverize in a food processor and let it settle to remove any air bubbles. Season with salt and pepper. **FRESH LEAVES AND COURGETTE FLOWER** / Mix the oil together with the açai powder. Divide the courgette flower into four pieces. Paint the leaves with the açai mixture.

PLATING / Cut the lobster in pieces and lightly coat with the mojo sauce. Sauté lightly on both sides in a frying pan with a drop of oil. Finish cooking the body and the claws in the salamander. Plate the lobster and drizzle a bit of the tomato pulp beside it. Place the leaves and the courgette flower on top of the tomato pulp. Set the crispy crepe on top. Sprinkle with sesame seeds. A waiter should serve the tomato water over the dish in the dining room.

PINEWOOD SQUAB

— Serves 4. —

MOJO SAUCE

40 g sautéed onion
15 g olive oil
60 g pine nuts
½ grilled tomato
15 g fried bread
100 g cola drink

SQUAB

2 squabs (525 g each)
Salt and powdered ginger
Liquorice root

SAUCE

2 squab carcasses
3 medium onions
4 leeks
2 dl oil
1 bouquet garni
2 tbsp Acacia honey

PINEAPPLE

200 g pineapple pulp
2.5 g kappa carrageenan

BLACK PINE NUTS

40 g pine nuts
2 tbsp ground black sesame seeds
250 g water

GARNISH

15 g black pine nuts
1 tsp Nigella seeds
10 g toasted pistachio nuts, broken into pieces
50 g peeled pineapple
50 g olive oil
8 leaves of fresh mint, chopped
2 tbsp rice vinegar
Salt and pepper

OTHER INGREDIENTS

freeze-dried barley grass and 25 g celery

MOJO SAUCE / Pulverize all the ingredients in a food processor to make a thick paste. **SQUAB** / Remove the squab breasts and season lightly. Generously coat with the mojo sauce and cook on a flat top grill or in a frying pan. Set aside. Save the carcasses for the sauce. **SAUCE** / Cut up the carcasses and brown them in a pan with a little oil. Chop the vegetables and use the remaining oil to sauté them in a separate pan until golden. Strain the vegetables, add to the carcasses and sauté well. Cover with water and allow to reduce. Strain and season. Add a few drops of oil at the end. **PINEAPPLE** / Pulverize the pulp and kappa powder and boil for 1 minute. Pour the pulp into pineapple-shaped silicone moulds and allow to cool. Unmould and scoop out a small portion. Fill with some of the mojo sauce. Set aside. **BLACK PINE NUTS** / Boil the pine nuts and sesame seeds in water for 20 minutes. If the pine nuts have not turned black, add a little more water and another pinch of sesame seeds and continue to reduce until they do. Remove the pine nuts and set aside. **GARNISH** / Make a vinaigrette by mixing the oil, vinegar and mint. Season with salt and pepper. Cut the pineapple into thin slices and toss together with the Nigella seeds, pistachios and black pine nuts. Serve separately in small bowls.

PLATING / Set the squab on the plate with the pineapple to one side. Finish the dish by sprinkling with barley grass, black pine nuts and thinly sliced celery. Serve the other garnishes on the side.

The moulds help us to represent reality and play with it. The pine aromas offer us the depth of flavour necessary to highlight the main ingredient.

—— *Pinewood squab* ——

BLACK
LEMONS

— Serves 4. —

SOUR LEMON

150 g lemon juice
2 lemon peels
2 eggs
2 egg yolks
100 g butter
50 g liquid glucose
50 g milk
Lemon-shaped silicone moulds

BLACK SHELL

50 g cocoa butter
250 g chocolate
3 g black powder colouring

WHEATGRASS LEAVES

50 g olive oil
15 g freeze-dried wheatgrass powder
1 sheet oven paper

OTHER INGREDIENTS

5 g black lemon (loomi) powder

SOUR LEMON / Mix all the ingredients thoroughly and bring to a boil. Pour into the moulds and freeze. **BLACK SHELL** / Melt the chocolate and cocoa butter. Add the colouring agent and mix well. Skewer each frozen sour lemon with a needle and dip in the black mixture just enough to thinly coat. Refrigerate for 3 hours. **WHEATGRASS LEAVES** / Cut the sheets of oven paper into four leaf shapes. Mix the oil and wheatgrass powder.

PLATING / Present each black lemon on a leaf painted with green wheatgrass oil. Sprinkle with some black lemon powder. Note: These black lemons, or loomi, are traditionally served in bamboo steamers.

WHITE TUNA
TAMALE

— Serves 4. —

MOJO

50 g sweetcorn kernels
25 g white wine
1 leek, pan grilled
50 g roasted almonds
25 g rhubarb jam
1 g freeze-dried barley grass
10 g lemon juice
Salt and pepper

TUNA BELLY

400 g cleaned tuna belly, with skin
Pinch of lemon zest
Salt and powdered soursop

TUNA BELLY DRESSING

10 g walnuts
10 g sunflower seeds
10 g sweetcorn kernels
100 g olive oil

WINE-STAINED CORN HUSKS

4 corn husks
2000 g red wine

PURPLE SAUCE

1 onion
1000 g water
2 g Xantana
1 tsp shiso vinegar
Salt and pepper

FRUIT AND NUT BASE

2 g chives, finely chopped
2.5 g freeze-dried corn
5 g freeze-dried pineapple
2.5 g freeze-dried red pepper
25 g roasted almonds
2.5 g freeze-dried raspberries
70 g orange juice
10 g sugar

CRISPY SHISHO LEAVES

50 g water
50 g sugar
4 red shiso leaves

OTHER INGREDIENTS

2 additional red shiso leaves, julienned

MOJO / Pulverize all ingredients in a food processor. Season with salt and pepper and add a pinch of sugar. **TUNA BELLY** / Cut the tuna belly into rectangles. Season to taste, add the soursop and lemon zest, and set aside. **TUNA BELLY DRESSING** / Pulverize all ingredients in a food processor and set aside. **WINE-STAINED CORN HUSKS** / Boil the corn husks for a few minutes. Drain and cover with red wine. Store at room temperature for 48 hours. Drain and let dry at 55°C. **PURPLE SAUCE**/ Julienne the onion and add water. Cook over low heat until the liquid reduces by half. Strain and thicken with Xantana. Add vinegar and season with salt and pepper. **FRUIT AND NUT BASE** / Mix the juice with the sugar and add to the rest of the ingredients. Spread the mixture between two sheets of oven paper. Store in a dry place for 4 hours, then remove the paper and cut into a square. **CRISPY SHISHO LEAVES** /Boil the water and sugar together for 2 minutes. When cool, dip the leaves in the syrup and let dry on a silicone mat.

PLATING / Sear the tuna belly with a drop of oil on the skin side only. Remove from heat, spread with the mojo sauce, and finish cooking on a flat top grill or in a salamander grill, adding a bit of the dressing. Plate the fruit and nut base and place the tuna belly to the side. Top with both the julienned and the crispy shiso leaves. Cover the arrangement with the corn husks and sauce the plate.

TERPENE SQUAB

— Serves 4. —

MOJO SAUCE

100 g ground almonds
1 drop eucalyptus oil
50 g peeled orange segments
1 sautéed onion
1 tbsp olive oil
1 tbsp lemon juice
Salt and pepper

SQUAB

2 squab pigeons (525 g each)
Salt, powdered ginger and
liquorice root

SQUAB SAUCE

2 squab carcasses
3 medium onions
4 leeks
1 bouquet garni
200 g oil
Salt and pepper

SAUCE INFUSION

The zest of ¼ lemon
5 g fresh ginger
1 lemon leaf
Pine needles (Pinus radiata)
2 cloves

GARNISH

80 g peeled watermelon
4 mint leaves
2 egg whites
2 tsp sugar
Pinch of thyme
Powdered ginger
Salt and pepper

OTHER INGREDIENTS

segments of ½ orange and ½ lemon,
finely julienned zest of ¼ lime, new
mint leaves, finely julienned candied
ginger, 2 cloves black garlic, 4 fried
almonds and lemon verbena leaves

MOJO SAUCE / Blend all the ingredients to make a thick paste. **SQUAB** / Remove the squab breasts and season lightly. Generously coat with the mojo and cook on a flat top grill or in a frying pan. Set aside. Save the carcasses for the sauce. **SAUCE** / Cut up the carcasses and brown them in a pan with a little oil. Chop the vegetables and use the remaining oil to sauté them in a separate pan until golden. Strain the vegetables, add to the carcasses and sauté well. Cover with water and allow to reduce. Strain and season. Add a few drops of oil at the end. **SAUCE INFUSION** / Chop up all the ingredients evenly and place in a tea filter. Set aside. **GARNISH** / Beat the egg whites with the sugar. Arrange the mint leaves on a silicone mat on a baking tray and brush with the egg and sugar mixture. Bake for 14 minutes at 150°C. Remove and store in a dry place until needed. Cut the watermelon into cubes and season with salt and pepper. Sprinkle with ginger and add a pinch of thyme. Present the watermelon cubes with the mint leaves when serving.

PLATING / Arrange the squab on the plate. Accompany with some orange and lemon segments, lime zest, mint leaves, candied ginger, lemon verbena, black garlic and chopped, fried almonds. Remove the sauce infusion filter at the table and serve the sauce sparingly over the dish. Serve the garnish separately.

LADYBIRD LADYBIRD

— Serves 4. —

LADYBIRD FILLING

150 g natural yogurt
150 g white chocolate

LADYBIRD COATING

200 g water
3.5 g kappa carrageenan
1.2 g cochineal food colouring

BLACK SPOTS

8 g liquorice paste
75 g water
1 g kappa carrageenan

OLIVE OIL CARAMEL SAUCE

100 g sugar
3 tbsp extra virgin olive oil

◇◇

LADYBIRD FILLING / Beat the natural yogurt well with a whisk. Melt the chocolate, keeping the temperature below 35ºC. Combine both ingredients and allow to set for 24 hours in the freezer. Shape quenelles with the mixture using two dessert spoons. Store in the freezer until needed. **LADYBIRD COATING** /Boil all the ingredients for one minute and pulverize. Use a hypodermic needle to paint the frozen 'ladybirds' with a thin film of the coating. Set aside. **BLACK SPOTS** / Mix the liquorice paste in water and bring to a boil. Strain, add the kappa powder and pulverize in a food processor. Use a dropper to drop spots of the black mixture onto a silicone mat. Set aside. **OLIVE OIL CARAMEL SAUCE** / Caramelize the sugar to a deep golden brown. Pour it out on a tray and let cool. Pulverize it in a professional blender. Add the oil and mix well just before serving.

PLATING / Place the black dots on the surface of the ladybirds. On a bowl that represents a plate of flowers, place the ladybirds and pour the olive oil caramel sauce around it.

Few insects overcome the apprehension caused by their presence among us. One of them is the ladybird. To taste it, you must first look among the flowers.

— Ladybird, ladybird —

SEA BREAM
WITH NASTURTIUM LEAVES

— Serves 4. —

SEA BREAM MARINADE

1 seabream (600 g)
250 g white wine vinegar
250 g brandy
200 g olive oil (0.4%)
½ tbsp whole grain mustard
Salt

CHERRY MOJO SAUCE

1 ripe tomato
30 g fried almonds
60 g cherries, pitted
30 g soaked bread
3 tbsp sherry vinegar
½ tbsp wholegrain mustard
Salt and ginger powder

SWEET PAPRIKA OIL

100 g olive oil
10 g sweet paprika

FRUIT SAUCE

1 tbsp passion fruit pulp
1 tbsp mango pulp
4 tbsp extra virgin olive oil

OTHER INGREDIENTS

Nasturtium leaves, extra virgin olive oil
and sweet paprika

SEA BREAM MARINADE / Clean and fillet the fish removing all bones. Salt the fillets, soak them in vinegar for 40 minutes, and drain. Soak them in the brandy for another 30 minutes. Drain and cover in olive oil for 2 hours. Cut the fish into cubes and coat with the mustard. **CHERRY MOJO SAUCE** / Lightly blanche the tomato, and peel. Cut into slices and fry in a tablespoon of hot oil just enough to take out the raw edge. Add all the ingredients to a food processor and pulverize until smooth. Season with salt and a pinch of ginger powder. **SWEET PAPRIKA OIL** / Mix the ingredients and allow the oil to settle. Set aside. **FRUIT SAUCE** / Combine all the ingredients and mix well.

PLATING / Spread a spoonful of the cherry mojo on the plate and drizzle with some of the sweet paprika oil. Arrange a few pieces of sea bream on the base, as seen in the photograph, and top with a few lightly salted nasturtium leaves. Decorate the plate with a few splashes of the fruit sauce and lightly sprinkle with sweet paprika.

SEABERRY MILK POT

— Serves 4. —

SEABERRY COULIS

75 g yellow seaberry pulp
1 egg
1 egg yolk
60 g sugar
50 g butter
25 g liquid glucose
25 g milk

SMOKED MILK

200 g sheep's milk
15 g sugar
0.7 g Xantana

PRALINE PEANUTS

200 g peanuts
120 g sugar
75 g water

CHERRY BANANA CHIPS

½ plantain
120 g cherry pulp
200 g olive oil (for frying)
20 g confectioner's sugar

SWEET POTATO CHIPS

1 small sweet potato
200 ml olive oil (for frying)
Salt

SEABERRY COULIS / Boil all the ingredients, stirring continuously. Pulverize in a blender and cover the bottom of each pot with a thin layer of coulis. Let cool and set aside. **SMOKED MILK** / Smoke the milk in a smoker for 15 minutes. Pulverize the milk with the sugar and Xantana and allow to settle. **PRALINE PEANUTS** / Put the sugar and water in a pan and bring to a boil. Keep stirring with a spatula until the temperature reaches 117°C. Remove from the heat and add the peanuts, stirring continuously until the caramel sticks. Put the pan back on the heat and keep stirring until the peanuts are fully caramelized. Spread them out on greaseproof paper to cool. Store in a dry place. **CHERRY BANANA CHIPS** / Peel the plantain and cut into thin slices. Leave the slices in the cherry pulp for 2 hours. Drain and pat dry with some kitchen paper. Heat the oil and fry the plantain slices. Drain well and dust with confectioner's sugar. **SWEET POTATO CHIPS** / Cut the sweet potato and slice finely. Heat the oil and fry the chips. Drain well and season with salt.

PLATING / Put 2 tablespoons of smoked milk over the seaberry coulis in each of the four pots. Decorate with a few praline peanuts and cherry banana chips.

LICENCE TO KRILL

— Serves 4. —

SCARLET SHRIMP TAILS

8 scarlet shrimp tails
4 mint leaves
4 sprigs of dill
4 g lemongrass
25 g extra virgin olive oil
Salt and pepper
Powdered ginger

MOJO SAUCE

1 boiled onion
50 g beetroot juice
20 g tomato purée
1 peeled tomato
100 g toasted almonds
1 fried garlic clove, peeled
50 g olive oil
Salt, pepper and sugar

GREEN KRILL CRACKERS

25 g krill
6 shrimp tails
1 g spirulina
1 g phytoplankton
12 g water

SAUTÉED VEGETABLES

2 baby courgettes
6 spinach leaves
2 cabbage leaves
½ avocado
Juice of ½ lemon
Salt and pepper
2 tbsp olive oil

OTHER INGREDIENTS

krill oil, 250 g olive oil and Yka leaves

SCARLET SHRIMP TAILS / Season the shrimp tails with salt, pepper and a pinch of ginger. Place them in a vacuum bag with the remaining ingredients. Bag at 80% vacuum and refrigerate for 3 hours. **MOJO SAUCE** / Pulverize all the ingredients in a food processor. Season with salt, pepper and sugar to taste. **GREEN KRILL CRACKERS** / Pulverize the shrimp tails with the krill. Roll the mixture out between two 10 × 10 cm sheets of oven paper. Repeat the steps to make 4 crackers. Dehydrate at 60ºC. Remove the sheets of paper and brush the crackers with the spirulina, water and phytoplankton mixture. Store in the dehydrator until ready to use. **SAUTÉED VEGETABLES** / Finely dice the courgettes, spinach leaves and cabbage. Sauté in the oil. Season. Just before serving, scoop out some avocado balls with a small melon baller. Sprinkle with lemon juice and set aside until needed.

PLATING / Just before serving, lightly fry the crackers. Drain over something round like potatoes or oranges to keep their shape. To serve, arrange some lightly oiled Yka leaves on the plate and brush the plate with some mojo sauce. Place the sautéed vegetables, grilled scarlet shrimps coated in mojo and the avocado balls on top. Cover with the cracker and drizzle with some krill oil.

PRAWNS AND CHARRED LEMONS WITH PATCHOULI

— Serves 4. —

CHARRED LEMONS

4 medium-sized lemons

LEMON MOJO SAUCE

100 g toasted almonds
10 g choricero pepper pulp
20 g toast (well toasted)
20 g Isomalt sugar
35 g olive oil
5 drops lemon juice
Salt, pepper and powdered ginger

GRILLED PRAWNS

12 Palamós prawns
Salt and pepper
Powdered ginger

CHICKEN AND FENNEL BROTH

1 clean chicken (750 g)
1 tbsp olive oil (0.4%)
2.5 kg water
1 g Xantana (per ½ litre of stock)
4 sprigs of fennel
Salt and pepper

VULCANO POWDER

15 g sugar
1 g charred aubergine powder
1 g powdered cinnamon
1 well-toasted corn tortilla

GINGER OIL

100 g olive oil (0.4%)
50 g peeled fresh ginger

OTHER INGREDIENTS

patchouli essential oil and a few sprigs of fennel

CHARRED LEMONS / Clean well and grill over hot coals until charred. Do not allow to burn. **LEMON MOJO SAUCE** / Grind all the ingredients together in a food processor. Season with salt, pepper and ginger. **GRILLED PRAWNS** / Separate the heads from the tails and peel. Season the tails with salt, pepper and a little ginger. Dip them lightly in the mojo sauce and grill the tails and heads over charcoal. Set aside. **CHICKEN AND FENNEL BROTH** / Lightly season the chicken, rub with oil and place in a roasting tin. Roast for one hour at 190°C. When the chicken is cooked, collect the juices from the roasting pan and reduce by half. Strain and reserve. Put the chicken in a pan and cover with water. Leave to simmer for 4 hours over low heat. Next, strain the broth and thicken slightly with the correct ratio of Xantana. Season the fennel and infuse in the broth for 4 minutes. Strain and set aside. **VOLCANO POWDER** / Pulverize all the ingredients in a food processor. **GINGER OIL** / Pulverize the oil and ginger. Strain.

PLATING / Hollow out the lemons without perforating the shell. Coat the inside of the lemon with the mojo sauce and add the grilled prawns. Drizzle with a little ginger oil and add a spoonful of the chicken and fennel broth. Place one prawn-filled lemon on each plate. Rub the outside of the lemons lightly with the aromatic patchouli oil. Garnish with the volcano powder and a sprig of fennel. Present the prawn heads in a small bowl with the roast chicken juices and a few drops of ginger oil.

Grilling lemons on a barbecue, directly over coals, is a curious way of extracting the scents and nuances that remain locked inside. Accompany thcm with the subtle marine touch in the form of seaweed, which enhances and emphasizes the seafood base.

—— Prawns and charred lemons with patchouli ——

RADIANT ANTHOCYANIN DUCK

— Serves 4. —

MOJO SAUCE

½ onion, sautéed
50 g red wine
1 clove fried garlic
15 g caramelized pecan nuts
15 g toasted almonds
Powdered ginger
Salt and pepper

DUCK

2 wild ducks
Salt, powdered ginger and liquorice root

SAUCE

2 duck carcasses
3 medium onions
4 leeks
1 bouquet garni
200 g olive oil
Chopped chives and the fat rendered from the bones
Salt and pepper

ACIDIC ANTHOCYANINS

125 g hibiscus stock (see hibiscus jam recipe)
35 g sugar
0.5 g Xantana
5 g mango, peeled and chopped

SWEET NOTES

50 g red wine
25 g sugar
0.5 g Xantana
50 g chopped grapes

HIBISCUS JAM

50 g dried hibiscus
1000 g water
125 g sugar
0.5 g Xantana

OTHER INGREDIENTS

small mint leaves and juniper berries

MOJO SAUCE / Pulverize all the ingredients in a food processor to make a thick paste. Season with salt, pepper and a hint of ginger. Set aside. **DUCK** / Remove the duck breasts and season lightly. Generously coat the breasts with the mojo and cook on a flat top grill or in a frying pan. Set aside. Save the carcasses for the sauce. **SAUCE** / Cut up the carcasses and brown them in a pan with a little oil. Chop the vegetables and use the remaining oil to sauté them in a separate pan until golden. Strain the vegetables, add to the carcasses and sauté well together. Cover with water and allow to reduce. Strain and season. Add a few drops of oil and the chopped chives at the end. **ACIDIC ANTHOCYANINS** / Pulverize all the ingredients, except for the chopped mango, in a food processor. Add the mango and bring to a boil. Set aside. **SWEET NOTES** / Pulverize all the ingredients, except for the chopped grapes, in a food processor. Bring to a boil and add the grapes. Set aside. **HIBISCUS JAM** / Cook the hibiscus leaves in water for 2 hours over low heat. Strain the broth and set aside. Add the sugar and finish the jam. Mix the broth with the Xantana (0.5 g Xantana to 125 g broth) and let sit.

PLATING / Arrange the sliced duck breasts on the plates and sauce around it, keeping each flavour separate.

BAMBOO AND KOKOTXAS

— *Serves 4.* —

MOJO SAUCE

50 g olive oil
1 small roasted tomato
1 roasted spring onion
25 g toasted almonds
1 clove fried garlic
Dash of sherry vinegar
1 drop orange-blossom water
Salt and pepper

KOKOTXAS

12 kokotxas
Salt

BAMBOO LEAVES

8 bamboo leaves
1 tbsp olive oil

PAINTED DRESSING

10 g truffle juice
10 g sherry vinegar
40 g extra virgin olive oil
Salt and powdered ginger

BAMBOO SHOOTS

50 g pickled bamboo shoots
80 g olive oil
15 g lemon juice
Salt and pepper

OTHER INGREDIENTS

8 shelled hazelnuts and hazelnut oil

MOJO SAUCE / Pulverize all the ingredients except the vinegar and orange-blossom water in a food processor. Adjust the salt and pepper and add a splash of vinegar and orange-blossom water. **KOKOTXAS** / Rinse the kokotxas well and season with salt and pepper. Just before serving, brush lightly with the mojo and cook both sides very lightly on a flat top grill or in a frying pan with a little oil. **BAMBOO LEAVES** / Brush with olive oil. **PAINTED DRESSING** / Mix together all the ingredients. **BAMBOO SHOOTS** / Cut the pickled bamboo into small pieces and mix with the other ingredients. Let stand for 15 minutes.

PLATING / Brush a bamboo leaf lengthwise with the painted dressing and arrange the kokotxas along the brushstroke. Add the bamboo shoots. Spoon a little dressing over the cheeks and top with sliced hazelnuts. Add a touch of hazelnut oil. Cover with another bamboo leaf.

HAZELNUT PARFAIT
WITH DRIED STRAWBERRIES

— Serves 4. —

HAZELNUT PARFAIT
25 g water
110 g sugar
110 g egg yolks
200 g hazelnut praline
25 g light cream
2 sheets gelatin (4 g)
350 g lightly whipped cream

DRIED STRAWBERRIES
8 strawberries
200 ml grapeseed oil

COCONUT JUICE
100 g coconut milk
75 g simple syrup
0.5 g Xantana

RASPBERRY DROPS
25 g raspberry pulp
25 g simple syrup

OTHER INGREDIENTS
Green tea powder

HAZELNUT PARFAIT/ Heat the sugar and water to 120°C. Beat the egg yolks and mix in the syrup. Keep the mixture as stiff as possible. Heat the light cream to dissolve the gelatin and add to the egg yolk mixture. Finally, fold in the lightly whipped cream very carefully so no air is lost. Pour into four rectangular non-stick silicone moulds and freeze. **DRIED STRAWBERRIES** / Blanch the strawberries in boiling water for 40 seconds. Place them on a silicone mat and dehydrate for 24 hours at 55°C. Store in oil until needed. **COCONUT JUICE** / Pulverize all the ingredients and leave to rest in the refrigerator for 2 hours. **RASPBERRY DROPS** / Pulverize both ingredients. Set aside.

PLATING / Remove the hazelnut parfait from the freezer and unmould. Coat the sides with the green tea powder. Leave on a plate until it becomes room temperature. Drain the dried strawberries and arrange around the parfait. Add some coconut juice and raspberry drops to complete the dish.

FISH OUT
OF WATER

— Serves 4. —

MOJO SAUCE

3 boiled garlic cloves
20 g liquefied parsley
10 g apple cider vinegar
100 g olive oil
50 g fried almonds
10 g toasted bread
1 g veronica (aka speedwell, bird's eye, or
gypsyweed)
Salt and pepper

HAKE

4 hake loins (125 g each)
Salt

GREEN VIZCAINA SAUCE

100 g green sauce (salsa verde)
100 g traditional vizcaina sauce
1 g veronica
5 g lime juice
30 g extra virgin olive oil
Salt and pepper

FRIED SPHERES

450 g fish stock
5 g freeze-dried barley grass
50 g parsley juice
4 balloons
72 sheets oblaat (15 x 15 cm)
4 tbsp olive oil (0.4%)
Olive oil for frying

GARLIC

12 garlic cloves
1000 g milk

OTHER INGREDIENTS

100 g green sauce

MOJO SAUCE / Mix all the ingredients and pulverize. Season with salt and pepper. **HAKE** / Spread the hake with the mojo sauce and cook the fillets on a flat top grill or in a frying pan without cooking all the way through. Set aside. **GREEN VIZCAINA SAUCE** / Boil the green sauce together with the vizcaina sauce and the veronica. Add the lime juice and olive oil at the last minute. Season with salt and pepper. **FRIED SPHERES** / Bring the fish broth to a boil. Remove from the heat and infuse the barley grass in the broth. Allow to cool and add the parsley juice. Mix well and strain. Pour the liquid into a spray bottle. Inflate the balloons and paint with olive oil. Cover the surface of the balloon with the oblaat sheets. Spray the balloon with the liquid and cover with another layer of oblaat sheets. Repeat this operation 18 times. Hang the spheres on a string to dry for 2 hours. Carefully prick the balloons, leaving an empty sphere. Place the spheres on a cooking rack and brush with hot oil. **GARLIC** / Simmer the whole garlic cloves in three changes of milk and confit over low heat. Season lightly.

PLATING / Finish cooking the hake in the green sauce. Place a piece of the hake on the plate surrounded by the green vizcaina sauce and garlic. Cover the fish with the sphere to hold in the aromas and add a touch of crispness when broken.

You feel like a child when a game involving papier-mâché becomes an edible dome on which you can smoke a product and present it in an amazing way.

—— Fish out of water ——

VEAL STEW
WITH 'INK'

— Serves 4. —

VEAL CHEEKS

2 veal cheeks
100 g olive oil (0.4%)
2 onions
2 leeks
2 shallots
2 carrots
1 glass of brandy
250 g port wine
250 g red wine
1 vanilla bean
25 g pineapple
250 g beef broth
Water
Salt

VEAL AND SESAME SAUCE

200 g veal cheek juice
80 g black sesame

PARSLEY YOGHURT

100 g plain yogurt
15 g sugar
Chopped parsley
Salt and pepper

OTHER INGREDIENTS

Flowers and microgreens

VEAL CHEEKS / Clean and julienne the vegetables. Sauté them over low heat in half the oil. Season the cheeks and sear them over high heat in the rest of the oil. Once golden, remove the oil and flambé with the brandy. Add the port and red wine and reduce. Add the pulp from the vanilla bean and the pineapple. Next, add the vegetables and continue to sauté. Add half of the broth and an equal amount of water to cover the cheeks. Cook over low heat until the meat is practically falling apart. Remove from the broth and allow to cool. Cut the cheeks into thick triangular pieces. Boil the vegetables in the broth. Remove the vanilla and pineapple. Pulverize and strain. **VEAL AND SESAME SAUCE** / Combine both ingredients and cook for 15 minutes over low heat. Strain and adjust salt. **PARSLEY YOGHURT** / Combine all the ingredients and mix well.

PLATING / Heat the meat in the veal and sesame sauce just before serving. Put a tablespoon of parsley yogurt in the centre of the dish and place the sliced veal on top. Spoon sauce over the top. Garnish with flowers and microgreens.

PISTACHIO STONE
AND CITRUSY BEETROOT

— Serves 4. —

PISTACHIO STONE

250 g pistachio butter
40 g cocoa butter

RED LEMON SKIN

2 lemons
500 g beetroot juice
250 g sugar

RED LEMON

2 peeled lemons
200 g liquified beetroots
100 g sugar

CITRUS ZEST

1 lemon
1 lime

OTHER INGREDIENTS

grated lemon and lime zest, candied pistachios

PISTACHO STONE / Vacuum-seal the pistachio butter with the cocoa butter and heat in a water bath at 60ºC until the mixture is melted. Pour the mixture into a whipped cream dispenser, charge with two nitrous oxide canisters, and fill a rectangular silicone pastry mould to 85%. Allow to cool. **RED LEMON SKIN** / Peel the lemons including the inner white layer of the skin. Blanch the lemon peel four times in boiling water and drain well. Pack the peels in a vacuum bag along with the beetroot juice and sugar. Cook in a water bath for 4 hours at 60ºC. Let cool inside the bag. **RED LEMON** / Separate the lemon segments and remove all peel, pith and membranes. Seal the lemon wedges with the beetroot juice and sugar in a vacuum bag, and chill for 24 hours. Cook in a water bath for 20 minutes at 60ºC. **CITRUS ZEST** / At the last moment, grate the peel of both citrus fruits.

PLATING / Portion the pistachio stone and square the edges. Place on a pool of the red lemon juice. Garnish the plate with the lemon pieces and sprinkle citrus zest over the top.

ON A RAZOR'S EDGE

— Serves 4. —

RAZOR CLAMS

8 razor clams
Salt

TOMATO GEL

60 g tomato sauce
4 cherry tomatoes
2 tbsp water
2 g Xantana
Salt and pepper
A pinch of sugar

GREEN MAYONNAISE

120 g sunflower oil
25 g extra virgin olive oil
1 egg
50 ml parsley broth
1 tsp vinegar
1 tsp phytoplankton
Salt

FRIED BACON

60 g bacon

OTHER INGREDIENTS

A pinch of nori powder, chopped chives and extra virgin olive oil

---

RAZOR CLAMS / Soak the clams in salt water for a few hours to purge them of any sand. Rinse well. Grill the clams on a flat top grill or in a frying pan with a little oil for 1 minute on each side. Remove the meat from the shell and cut it into 3 pieces. Leave them on the grill for 1 to 2 minutes before removing from the heat. Add garlic and parsley. Serve hot. **TOMATO GEL** / Combine the tomato sauce, cherry tomatoes and water and pulverize until smooth. Strain and pulverize again with the Xantana. Season with salt and pepper and add a pinch of sugar if needed. **GREEN MAYONNAISE** / Combine all the ingredients, except the oil, in the bowl of a professional blender and process until creamy. Slowly add the oil to create an emulsion. Salt to taste. Place the mayonnaise in a siphon (½ litre) with a gas cartridge and shake well. Keep chilled until ready to use. **FRIED BACON** / Cut the bacon into small pieces and fry until crisp. Drain off all excess grease.

PLATING / Dab a bit of mayonnaise on the clam shell. On top, lay the pieces of clam, together with a spoonful of the tomato gel. Top with a few drops of extra virgin olive oil, bacon bits, chopped chives and a pinch of nori powder.

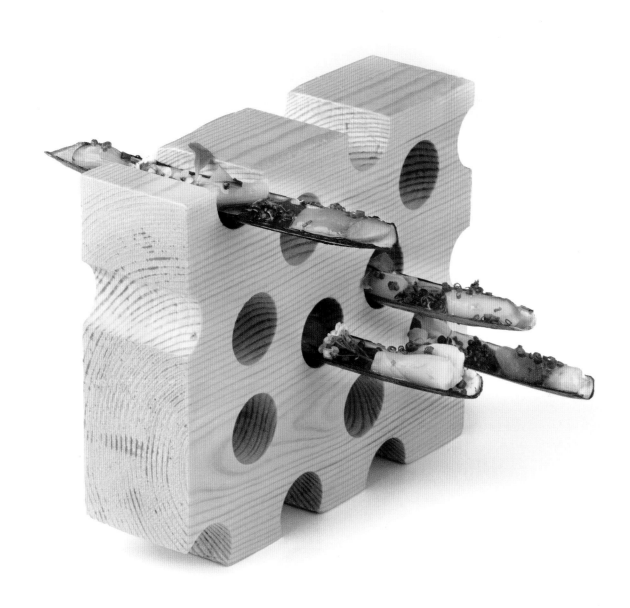

FLAMING CHICKPEA STEW

— Serves 4. —

'CHICKPEA' COFFEE*

500 g milk
175 g sugar
20 g decaffeinated coffee
0.5 g Xantana
1 gelatin sheet (2 g)
6 egg yolks
200 g cream

*For this step, you'll need a chickpea-shaped silicone mould

FLAMING LIQUEUR

150 g white rum
30 g sugar
20 g sesame paste
0.2 g Xantana
15 g alcohol

RUSTY NAILS

200 g cardamom infusion
50 g sugar
3 g gellan gum
15 g cocoa powder
2 g clove powder
A nail-shaped silicone mould

CHICKPEA SAND

40 g dried chickpeas
80 g sugar
3 tbsp water

'CHICKPEA' COFFEE / Combine the milk and 135 g sugar and bring to a boil. Pour over the coffee and leave to infuse. Mix in the Xantana, gelatin (previously soaked), and egg yolks. Make a crème anglaise with the mixture and allow to cool. Lightly whip the cream and remaining sugar. Carefully fold in the crème anglaise and pour into the chickpea mould. Freeze. **LIQUEUR** / Mix the ingredients together. **RUSTY NAILS** / In a saucepan, mix the cardamom infusion, sugar, gellan gum, and 10 g of cocoa powder. Boil over low heat for 2 minutes. Pour into the mould and allow to cool. Once cool, carefully unmould and coat in a mixture of cocoa and clove powder. **CHICKPEA SAND** / Grind the chickpeas without pulverizing them completely. Combine all ingredients, preferably in a semi-spherical pot, and heat to 115°C. Remove from heat and stir continuously until the sugar begins to solidify and cover the pieces of chickpeas. Keep stirring until the pieces are all separate; there will be sugar remaining in the bottom of the saucepan. Put the pan back on the heat to caramelize the sugar. Stir continuously and then pour onto a sheet of oven paper, separating all the pieces before the caramel cools.

PLATING / Place the coffee on the plate with the sand to one side and the nails scattered around it. Heat the ingredients for the liqueur in a small pitcher, which the server will flambé tableside, adding the chickpeas at the end.

The visual enchantment of fire. Textures melting to create sweet sensations over a vegetable stew.

— Flaming chickpea stew —

EMPANADILLAS

— Serves 4. —

FILLING

100 g milk
100 g cream
1 gelatin sheet (2 g)
100 g dark chocolate (52%)

PASTRY

80 g sugar
180 g sugar cane honey
1 stiffly beaten egg white
300 g ground almonds
Pinch of parsley powder
Pinch of Manuka honey powder

SOUR SAUCE

1 tamarillo fruit
Juice of ½ lemon
50 g sugar
100 g orange juice
0.5 g cochineal food colouring
1 g Xantana

OTHER INGREDIENTS

roasted walnuts, julienned orange peel
and rings of dried black olives

FILLING / Boil the milk and cream. Dissolve the pre-soaked gelatin in the hot mixture and pour it over the chocolate. Mix well until smooth and allow to cool. Set aside. **PASTRY** / Heat the sugar and honey to 120°C. Remove from the heat and fold in the beaten egg white. Add the ground almonds and mix thoroughly over a gentle heat. Roll out the pastry between two sheets of oven paper and cut out eight circles with a round cookie cutter. Place some of the filling in the middle and fold over, crimping the edges to create the empanadilla half-moon shape. Dust with the parsley and Manuka powders. **SOUR SAUCE** / Peel the tamarillo and chop up the pulp. Mix together with the remaining ingredients.

PLATING / Place two empanadillas on each plate, adding a little of the sauce to one side. Decorate the plate with the walnuts, julienned orange peel, and dried black olives.

ANISE AND APPLE
ROSQUILLAS

— Serves 4. —

APPLE RINGS

½ kg Reinette apples
85 g sugar
50 g cider
Pinch of powdered star anise

COATING

250 g cocoa butter
50 g milk chocolate

MACADEMIA AND YUZU SAUCE

250 g milk
100 g cream
½ star anise
15 g Amaretto liqueur
2 toasted macadamia nuts
2 egg yolks
75 g sugar
30 g cider
Yuzu essence

GLAZE

20 g egg white
100 g confectioner's sugar
5 g Anise liqueur

OTHER INGREDIENTS

A few drops of Amaretto liqueur, 1 fried macadamia nut and powdered star anise

APPLE RINGS / Core the apples and arrange on a baking tray. Sprinkle with the sugar, add the cider and dust with a pinch of star anise. Bake for 50 minutes at 200ºC. Pulverize and cool. Add the puréed apple to a piping bag, pipe the mixture into doughnut-shaped silicone moulds and put them in the freezer. When frozen, remove from the moulds and store in the freezer. **COATING** / Melt the cocoa butter and the chocolate together. Use a hypodermic needle to coat the frozen apple rings (rosquillas) with a thin layer of melted chocolate. Allow to set. **GLAZE** / Mix the glaze ingredients with a whisk until a smooth, white paste is formed. Allow the mixture to sit for 6 hours. **MACADEMIA AND YUZU SAUCE** / Combine the milk, cream, star anise, Amaretto and macadamia nuts in a saucepan and bring to a boil. Remove the star anise and pulverize the remaining ingredients in a blender. Press through a sieve. Mix the egg yolks, sugar, cider and a couple of drops of yuzu essence in a bowl. Combine both mixtures and heat gently to 80ºC to thicken the custard. Store in the refrigerator.

PLATING / Using a piping bag, cover the surface of each doughnut with a thin layer of the glaze. Arrange three or four apple doughnuts (depending on size) on each plate and sprinkle with some nuts. Serve a little macadamia and yuzu sauce on the side and add a few drops of Amaretto. Dust the plate with a pinch of powdered star anise.

'CORN ON THE COB' WITH TRUFFLES

— Serves 4. —

FOIE GRAS MIXTURE

180 g fresh foie gras
60 g cream cheese
2.5 g truffles
1 tbsp extra virgin olive oil
Ginger powder
Liquorice powder
30 g cocoa butter
Salt and black pepper
4 corn-on-the-cob silicone moulds

CORN OIL VINAIGRETTE

100 g corn oil
0.5 g cocoa powder
15 g confectioner's sugar
25 g late harvest Moscatel
1 tbsp grapefruit juice
Salt and pepper

COLOURED KERNELS

1 tbsp cooked yellow kernels
1 tbsp fresh raw yellow kernels
1 tbsp cooked black kernels
1 tbsp cooked white kernels
1 tbsp corn nuts

OTHER INGREDIENTS

freeze-dried figs and multicoloured fresh edible flowers

FOIE GRAS MIXTURE / Cut the foie gras into cubes and pan-fry. Allow to sit for 5 minutes and pulverize in a blender with the cheese, truffles and oil. Season the mixture and add some ground ginger and liquorice root. Melt the cocoa butter and brush a thin film on the corn-on-the-cob moulds. Wait until the butter hardens before filling the moulds with the foie gras mixture. Place in the refrigerator to set. Unmould and set aside. **CORN OIL VINAIGRETTE** /Combine all the ingredients and season with salt and pepper. **COLOURED KERNELS** / Cook each type of corn separately.

PLATING / Arrange the 'corn on the cob' in the middle of the plate and scatter the coloured kernels around the cob. Add the vinaigrette sparingly. Garnish with flowers and pieces of freeze-dried figs.

MONKFISH AT LOW TIDE

— Serves 4. —

MOJO SAUCE

1 onion
1 leek
100 g baked almonds
200 g rose water and jasmine tea
50 g olive oil (0.4%)
30 g Amarula liqueur
Salt, pepper and ginger

MONKFISH

1 kg monkfish
Salt

STARFISH

200 g concentrated fish fumet
50 g Curacao liqueur
1 g agar-agar
1 starfish mould

SOFT COCKLES

15 g butter
25 g olive oil
100 g onion, finely chopped
90 g carrot, finely chopped
40 g leek (white part only), finely chopped
80 g mussels, shelled
300 g mussel juice
1 g agar-agar
Salt and pepper
1 cockle-shaped mould

COCKLESHELLS

200 g mannitol
5 g nori seaweed powder
100 g olive oil
1 cockle-shaped mould

RED CODIUM SEAWEED

140 g water
110 g flour
30 g wheat bran
2 g cochineal food colouring
30 g Codium seaweed (tips only)
Olive oil for frying

PIQUILLO SAUCE

180 g piquillo peppers, seeded
½ garlic clove, chopped
2 tbsp olive oil
120 g water
5 g calcium salt
Salt and sugar

FOR THE PIQUILLO SAUCE SPHERES

Piquillo sauce
1000 g water
5 g sodium alginate*
100 g sunflower oil
*Sodium alginate is extracted from seaweed

SAUCE

300 g chicken broth
80 g fennel bulb
0.5 g Xantana
Salt and pepper

OTHER INGREDIENTS

Safflower powder

MOJO SAUCE / Clean the vegetables well and roast with a spoonful of olive oil. Pulverize all the ingredients in a food processor. Season with salt and pepper. **MONKFISH** / Clean and debone the monkfish. Portion. Season the fish with salt and brush with the mojo sauce. Grill lightly on the flat top grill without letting it take on too much colour. **STARFISH** / Heat the fumet and add the liqueur, then the agar-agar. Bring to a boil and pour the mixture into the moulds. Once cooled, remove the starfish from the moulds and set aside. **SOFT COCKLES** / Sauté the vegetables and simmer with the butter and olive oil. Once the vegetables are ready, add the cleaned mussels and sauté all together. Add the broth and agar-agar. Cook over low heat for 5 minutes. Season with salt and pepper. Pulverize the mixture in a food processor. Pour into the cockle-shaped moulds. **COCKLESHELLS** / Melt the mannitol and pour it over the mould. Let it stand for a few moments to take form and remove the rest. It is very important that the cockle form is very thin. Paint the shells with the oil and nori mixture. **RED CODIUM SEAWEED** / Combine all the ingredients in a bowl except for the seaweed and oil. Pulverize. Dip the seaweed tips in the mixture and fry at 190ºC until they just begin to take some colour. Drain well. **PIQUILLO SAUCE** / Fry the garlic in a pan with olive oil until golden. Add the piquillo peppers and sauté. Add the water and cook for 5 minutes. Pulverize in a food processor and strain. Season with salt and a touch of sugar. Add 5 g of calcium salt to 200 g of the piquillo mixture. Pulverize and let sit until the air bubbles have dissipated. **PIQUILLO SAUCE SPHERES** / Fully dissolve the sodium alginate in the water. Pulverize and refrigerate for 12 hours to eliminate air bubbles. Using a large syringe, drip the piquillo sauce mixture into the sodium alginate and water solution one drop at a time, making sure they do not stick together. Leave in the solution for 40 seconds. Use a slotted spoon to drain. Gently rinse in cold water, taking care not to break the spheres. Drain again and set aside in sunflower oil until ready to use. **SAUCE** / Cook the broth with the chopped fennel bulb for 5 minutes. Strain and add the Xantana. Pulverize to desired texture. Season with salt and pepper. **PLATING** / Paint the plate with the mojo sauce and place a monkfish fillet on top. Arrange the other elements around the fish. Sauce the monkfish lightly and sprinkle with safflower powder.

The iodized smell of the sea in a representation of moving water crashing into the rocks. A fish stranded on sand. Meanwhile, the waves appear to play to appear on the bottom of the plate.

ANOTHER BRICK IN THE CHOCOLATE AND MUSTARD WALL

— Serves 4. —

CHOCOLATE WALL

25 g water
110 g sugar
110 g whipped egg yolks
200 g dark chocolate (70%)
375 g semi-whipped cream

CRUNCHY OBLAAT AND MUSTARD

75 g orange juice
200 g sugar
50 g butter
150 g flour
15 g mustard
2.5 g mustard powder
8 oblaat sheets (10 x 10 cm)

FROZEN MANGO

2 ripe mangoes

CHOCOLATE WALL / Heat the water and the sugar to 120ºC. Add it to the previously whipped egg yolks. Keep the mixture well-whipped with high soft peaks. Melt the chocolate and add it to the yolk mixture. Add the whipped cream. This step should be done smoothly so that it doesn't lose texture and air. Pour into rectangular silicone moulds and freeze. **CRUNCHY OBLAAT AND MUSTARD** / Mix the orange juice with the sugar and butter. Then add the flour. Mix well. Add the mustard and mustard powder to 130 g of the orange juice and butter preparation. Mix well and let sit for 10 minutes in the refrigerator. Set 4 oblaat sheets on a silicone mat and brush with the mustard mixture. Cover each one with another oblaat sheet. Bake at 190ºC for 7 minutes. Remove them from the silicone mat and store in a dry place until ready to use. **FROZEN MANGO** / Peel the mangoes and chop them into medium-sized pieces. Freeze in a Pacojet beaker. Just before serving, pulverize the frozen mango twice in the Pacojet. Set aside.

PLATING/ Remove the chocolate wall from the freezer and let it stand for 2 minutes. Use a brick-shaped mould or a knife to score lines in the brickwork. Stand the 2 chocolate walls at an angle and place a frozen mango quenelle alongside and cover with the crispy mustard.

WHITE TUNA
AND RHUBARB

— Serves 4. —

MOJO SAUCE

50 g oil from a can of oil-packed tuna
5 g rehydrated dried lily flowers
Juice of ½ lemon
15 g rhubarb jam
25 g toasted, peeled sunflower seeds
½ slice of toasted cornbread
Salt and pepper

TUNA BELLY

400 g tuna belly with the skin on (scales removed)
Salt and powdered ginger

RHUBARB

1 piece of rhubarb (about 20 cm)
300 g water
100 g sugar
20 g lemon juice
100 g olive oil

LILY FLOWERS

10 g dehydrated lily flowers
1 tbsp cornflour
60 g water
Pinch of turmeric
Frying oil

FOR THE SAUCE

½ onion
1 medium sweet green Italian pepper
1 shallot
40 g butter
200 g beef consommé
5 g kaniwa seeds
Salt and pepper

MOJO SAUCE / Pulverize all the ingredients. Season and add sugar to taste. **TUNA BELLY** / Cut the belly into two even-sized rectangles. Smoke lightly for 4 minutes in a smoker. Season with salt and a little ginger. Cook the tuna with a drop of oil on a flat top grill, starting with skin side down. Remove the skin, coat the fish with the mojo and finish cooking on the flat top or under the grill. Cut each piece in two. Set aside. **RHUBARB** / Cut off a 10 cm length of rhubarb. Peel and cut lengthwise into thin sheets with a mandolin. Blanch in a syrup made with the water, sugar and lemon juice. Set aside. Cut the rest of the rhubarb diagonally into very thin slices with the mandolin. Keep in oil until needed. **LILY FLOWERS** / Mix the cornflour, water and tumeric in a bowl. Soak the lilies in water for an hour and remove the petals. Dip each petal into the batter. Heat the oil to 190°C and fry until lightly golden. Drain well. **SAUCE** / Finely chop the onion, green pepper and shallot and sauté in the butter. Add the consommé and simmer for 30 minutes on low heat. Pulverize and season with salt and pepper. Cook the kaniwa seeds for 2 minutes in a pan of boiling, salted water. Drain well and add to the sauce. Adjust the seasoning if necessary.

PLATING / Stand the fish upright on the plate and arrange a variety of rhubarb slices next to it. Sauce lightly and garnish with the lily flowers.

KUMQUATS WITH CAMU CAMU

— Serves 4. —

CRISP ORANGE BREAD

½ vanilla bean
200 g orange juice
40 g sugar
100 g cava
0.5 g camu camu powder
150 g day-old bread

KUMQUATS

12 kumquats
50 g water
100 g cava
100 g sugar

KUMQUAT FILLING

100 g orange juice
100 g sugar
50 g toasted almonds
25 g orange liqueur
6 egg yolks

CAMU CAMU SAUCE

150 g light cream
50 g sugar
1 g camu camu powder

OTHER INGREDIENTS

diced mango and mint leaves

CRISP ORANGE BREAD / Cut open the vanilla bean and place in a pan with the other ingredients except for the bread. Bring to a boil, turn off the heat and leave to infuse. Remove the crusts from the bread and cut into even-sized, irregular-shaped pieces. Moisten the pieces of bread in the infusion and dry in a dehydrator. Store in a dry place until ready to use. **KUMQUATS** / Cut the tops off the kumquats and hollow out the fruit. Keep the tops and save the pulp for other uses. Blanch the kumquats three times, changing the water each time. Drain and allow to cool. Next, make a syrup by boiling the water, cava and sugar together for 2 minutes. Let cool. Dip the blanched kumquats in the syrup and drain once more. Set aside. **KUMQUAT FILLING** / Combine all ingredients and pulverize. Heat the mixture gently, keeping it under 82°C. Cool over ice. Set aside. **CAMU CAMU SAUCE** / Pulverize the ingredients and set aside.

PLATING / Arrange the bread on the plate. Lay the stuffed kumquats (with tops) on top. Sauce sparingly and decorate with some mango and mint leaves.

CHOCOLATE FOREST

— Serves 4. —

TREE TRUNKS

75 g water
1 g konjac
0.45 g Xantana
0.6 g agar-agar
1 egg yolk
225 g dark couverture chocolate

COUVERTURE

225 g chocolate (72%)
60 g cocoa butter

FILLING

35 g orange juice
25 g sugar
15 g toasted almonds
10 g fried macadamia nuts
2 tbsp Cointreau
4 egg yolks
5 g passion fruit pulp

CHESTNUTS

60 g chestnuts
Frying oil
Salt

LIQUORICE SAUCE

75 g liquorice paste
20 g thyme-infused water

CARAMELIZED APPLES

1 apple, cut into 1 x 1 cm cubes
100 g mannitol

OTHER INGREDIENTS

Seasonal flower petals and Honey Cress

TREE TRUNKS / Bring the water to a boil and add the remaining ingredients except the chocolate. Mix well. Melt the chocolate and mix all the ingredients together. Spread the preparation between two sheets of oven paper. Chill until firm. Remove the paper and with the help of a paring knife, shape the chocolate into a hollow trunk. **COUVERTURE** / Melt the chocolate and add the melted cocoa butter. Dip the trunks in the melted mixture, drain slightly and set aside. **FILLING** / Finely chop the nuts. Mix all the ingredients together except the passion fruit. Heat the mixture to no more than 80°C. Remove from the heat, let sit for 5 minutes and stir in the passion fruit pulp. Cool and set aside. **CHESTNUTS** / Peel the chestnuts, cut them into thin slices and fry in hot oil. Drain excess oil and season.**LIQUORICE SAUCE** / Mix the ingredients together. Set aside. **CARAMELIZED APPLES** /Heat the mannitol until it liquifies. Dip the apple cubes one by one into the liquid. Set aside.

PLATING / Paint a brushstroke of the sauce on the plate. Place the trunk, filled with the chilled filling, on the plate and garnish with the remaining ingredients.

You have to play with chocolate to achieve the texture of a truffle on a log. The rest of the dish is part of the playful component, because it is nestled in a forest. Meanwhile, the rain falls.

— *Chocolate forest* —

DUCK AND GUITAR SHAVINGS

— *Serves 4.* —

MOJO SAUCE

50 g Armagnac
50 g orange, peeled
50 g pineapple, peeled
50 g roasted skinless peanuts
2 garlic cloves, fried
60 g crusty bread
20 g butter
1 g neroli
Salt and pepper

WILD DUCK

2 wild duck, cleaned
Salt, ginger and liquorice powder

SAUCE

2 duck carcasses
3 medium onions
4 leeks
1 pinch fresh thyme
1 pinch citronella
200 g olive oil (0.4%)
Duck fat rendered from the bones
Salt and pepper

CASSAVA CORKSCREW

200 g cassava
Frying oil
Salt

OTHER INGREDIENTS

Fresh wood shavings from a classical
guitar maker (cedar or cypress)

MOJO SAUCE / Pulverize all the ingredients, forming a thick paste. Season with salt and pepper. Set aside. **WILD DUCK** / Remove the breasts from the duck and season them lightly. Coat the breasts with the mojo and cook them on the grill. Set aside. Use the carcasses and rest of the parts for the sauce. **SAUCE** / Chop the carcasses and brown them in a pan with a bit of oil. Chop the vegetables and brown lightly in another pan, using the remaining oil. Drain the oil from the vegetables and add them to the browned carcasses. Sauté together with the thyme. Cover with water, reduce, strain, and season. Add a few drops of oil and a pinch of citronella. **CASSAVA CORKSCREW** / Cut the cassava into long, thin strips. Roll oven paper into a tube and wrap the cassava strips around it in a spiral fashion. Holding with tweezers, fry in oil until just cooked. Remove the corkscrews from the tube and season.

PLATING / Plate the sliced duck breasts with the cassava corkscrews and the sauce. Cover the dish with a metal latticed rack and sprinkle with the wood shavings. When serving, the guest will first smell the wood shavings. Then lift the rack to reveal the duck below.

GIANT CHOCOLATE TRUFFLE

— Serves 4. —

CHOCOLATE MOUSSE

50 g milk
½ sheet gelatin (1 g)
100 g dark chocolate
150 g lightly whipped cream

BREAD CUBES

12 cubes soft white bread (1 x 1 cm)
1 tsp sugar
1 tsp olive oil
1 tsp cocoa powder

GIANT TRUFFLE

40 g cola-flavoured cotton candy sugar
1 g kola nut powder (Cola acuminata)
5 g cocoa powder

COCOA SAUCE

100 g orange liqueur
30 g sugar
15 g cocoa
100 g water

CHOCOLATE CAKE

75 g dark chocolate
75 g butter
2 eggs
110 g sugar
¼ vanilla bean
0.5 g salt
45 g flour
8 g cocoa

CHOCOLATE MOUSSE / Bring the milk to a boil and add the previously soaked gelatin. Pour the milk over the finely chopped chocolate. Melt and allow to cool slightly. Gently fold into the whipped cream so that the mousse does not deflate. Keep chilled. **BREAD CUBES** / Sauté the bread cubes together with the sugar and oil. When the bread is crisp remove from heat and let cool. Coat with cocoa powder and set aside. **GIANT TRUFFLE** / Pour the sugar into a cotton candy machine until it makes a thread. Wrap it around the chocolate mousse, bread cubes and kola nut powder and form a ball. Coat with cocoa powder and set aside. **CHOCOLATE CAKE** / Melt the chocolate with the butter. Add the eggs, sugar, inside of the vanilla bean pod (save the rest for other uses) and salt. Mix well. Mix the flour and cocoa powder together and add to the chocolate mixture. Mix well. Spread on a baking sheet and bake for 25 minutes at 160ºC. Set aside. **COCOA SAUCE** / Mix all the ingredients and boil for 2 minutes over medium heat. Let cool.

PLATING / Roll out a piece of the cake between two pieces of oven paper until quite thin. Set it on the plate with the truffle on top. In the dining room, pour the sauce over the truffle in front of the guest so that a crater opens in the top to reveal the inside.

BABY SQUID WITH BLACK TOMATO

— Serves 4. —

*SQUID INK SAUCE

1 onion
2 green peppers
1 garlic clove
25 g olive oil
1 cuttlefish (300 g)
1 small tomato
½ glass of red wine
2500 g water
Salt

BABY SQUID

12 small line-caught squid
Pinch of chopped parsley
2 tbsp olive oil
Salt and ginger powder

MOJO SAUCE

20 g ginger, peeled and sliced
50 g walnuts, peeled
1 tbsp lime juice
20 mint leaves
30 g toasted bread
10 g chives
15 g brandy
Salt and pepper

PSYLLIUM SAUCE

50 g dried tomatoes
2 g sweet paprika
100 g olive oil
3 g psyllium powder
Juice of 1 lemon
Salt and pepper

BLACK TOMATO

2 medium tomatoes
Pinch of thyme
Salt, pepper and sugar
2 tbsp extra virgin olive oil
250 g squid ink sauce*

GREEN SQUID DESIGN

1 bunch of parsley
1 tsp olive oil
Salt
A squid stencil

SQUID INK SAUCE / Chop the onion, peppers and garlic in julienne and sauté everything in the oil. Meanwhile, clean the cuttlefish and separate the ink sacks. Chop the cuttlefish into medium-sized pieces.When the vegetables are soft, add the cuttlefish. Sauté everything together for 15 minutes. Add the roughly cut tomato and cook until it just begins to fall apart. Add the wine and let reduce. Add the ink previously diluted in water. Mix well and add water to cover. Cook for about 50 minutes over medium heat. Remove all the cuttlefish and grind the rest in a blender. Strain and season, using only the sauce. Save the cuttlefish for other recipes. **BABY SQUID** / Clean the squid thoroughly and separate the bodies from the tentacles. Save the ink, fins and tentacles to use in other recipes. Make two parallel cuts part-way down the wide end of the squid. Season and add a pinch of ginger, parsley and oil. Set aside. **MOJO SAUCE**/ Blanche the ginger twice in boiling water and cool in ice water. Combine all the ingredients in a blender and pulverize. Season with salt and pepper. **PSYLLIUM SAUCE** / Cut the tomatoes into small pieces and mix with the rest of the ingredients. Season with salt and pepper. **BLACK TOMATO** / Peel the tomatoes and cut them in half. Place them on a baking sheet and sprinkle with a pinch of thyme, sugar, salt and pepper. Finally, add the olive oil and place them in the oven for 4 hours at 140°C. Remove from the oven and cover the tomatoes with the hot squid ink sauce. Let sit for 3 hours. The tomatoes will be coated in black. **GREEN SQUID DESIGN** / Juice only the parsley leaves and strain them through a cheesecloth. Add the oil and salt. Mix well. Pour into a spray bottle.

PLATING / Quickly grill both sides of the squid on a flat top grill. On one side of the plate place the squid stencil and paint it with the parsley spray. Remove the stencil leaving the silhouette of the squid on the plate. Arrange a black tomato on one side and the squid on the other, placing a little mojo sauce at the base. Finish the dish by saucing lightly with the psyllium sauce.

MONKFISH CLEOPATRA

— Serves 4. —

MARINADE

100 g olive oil (0.4%)
1 garlic clove
1 lemon peel
1 g turmeric

MONKFISH

1 kg monkfish
Salt

HIEROGLYPHICS

250 g pumpkin, steamed and peeled
25 g chickpeas, cooked
*25 g lemon oil**
Salt and pepper

SAUCE

3 shallots
1 yellow pepper
2 tbsp olive oil
100 g pineapple, peeled
100 ml chicken stock
5 g Muscovado sugar
Salt and pepper

MOJO SAUCE

50 g pecan nut purée
50 g olive oil (0.4%)
30 g toasted bread
Salt and pepper

OTHER INGREDIENTS

Finely chopped chives and a stencil with different shaped hieroglyphs

RUINS

2 onions
1 tbsp demi-glace
1250 g water
10 g sugar
2 tbsp olive oil (0.4%)
30 g rice
5 g squid ink
Salt

*Heat ½ litre olive oil (0.4%) to 60°C and add the peel of 2 lemons. Remove from heat and let the oil infuse with the lemon peel for 48 hours at room temperature.

MARINADE / Mix all the ingredients together. Set aside. **MONKFISH** / Clean the monkfish, remove the bones and cut it into serving portions. Season and place in the marinade for 5 minutes. **HIEROGLYPHICS**/ Purée the mixture. Drain and season with salt and pepper. **SAUCE** / Julienne the shallots and the pepper and sauté in the oil. When the vegetables are soft, add the pineapple cubes. Sauté the mixture. Add the chicken stock and cook for 5 minutes.Purée, strain and season with salt and pepper. **MOJO SAUCE** / Purée the mixture. Season with salt and pepper. **RUINS** / Finely chop the onions and sauté in oil. Add the water, demi-glace and sugar. Bring to a boil and let simmer for 45 minutes on low heat. Purée the mixture. Separate 1200g of puréed stock and add the squid ink. Bring to a boil and cook the rice in the stock for 20 minutes. Purée and season lightly. Use this batter mixture to make thin waffles in a waffle iron. Keep in a dry place until ready to use.

PLATING / Cook the monkfish fillet on a flat top grill without browning it.
Draw a spoonful of the mojo sauce across the dish and plate the fish. Use the stencil to make the hieroglyphs on the other side. Sauce lightly just before serving.

The fun game of assigning a product not to a place but to a person, or also to a culture or a language. Imagination takes us on a journey to the end of the Nile. A reflection about the nature of flavours.

—— *Monkfish cleopatra* ——

EGGETARIAN

— Serves 4. —

EGGS

4 eggs (60 g each)
10 g Idiazabal cheese
4 g sacha inchi
50 g panko crumb
Olive oil for frying
Salt

PORT WINE CHEESE

50 g Idiazabal cheese
10 g port wine

SEASONED MILK CRISP

400 g full-fat milk
4 g Xantana
Pinch of pepper
Pinch of oregano
1 tbsp garlic oil

BLUE CHEESE EGGS

350 g milk
2 g Xantana
60 g Gorgonzola
2 g Gluco (reverse spherification agent)

EGG BATH

500 g water
2.5 g sodium alginate

SHEEP'S MILK JUNKET

200 g sheep's milk
0.7 g Iota carrageenan powder
3 drops rennet
1 g salt

CHEESE SAND

30 g Idiazabal cheese
100 g ground raw almonds

CHEESE LEAVES

4 Age leaves
10 g cheese
50 g olive oil

OTHER INGREDIENTS

a pinch of baobab powder

EGGS / Cook the eggs in 63°C water for 20 minutes. Allow to sit for a minute. Break the shell carefully, remove the egg and lay gently on a plate. Use a Microplane grater to grate the cheese and the sacha inchi. Mix with the panko crumbs. Roll the egg in the mixture and fry briefly at 200°C. **PORT WINE CHEESE** / Cut the cheese into triangles and cover with the port. Leave to marinate for 12 hours. **SEASONED MILK CRISP** / Emulsify the milk and Xantana by beating for 5 minutes. At the last minute, add the oil and a pinch of oregano and black pepper. Spread on greaseproof paper and dehydrate at 55°C for 24 hours. Cut into pieces. **BLUE CHEESE EGGS** / Pulverize all the ingredients in a food processor and let the mixture settle in the refrigerator for 6 hours to remove any air bubbles. **EGG BATH** /Dissolve the sodium alginate in the water. Pulverize and allow to settle in the refrigerator for 12 hours to remove air bubbles. Using a tablespoon, carefully drop spoonfuls of the blue cheese mixture into the sodium alginate and water solution, making sure the 'eggs' do not touch or stick to each other. Leave them in the solution for 3 minutes. Drain carefully with a slotted spoon and rinse in cold water. Set aside until later. **SHEEP'S MILK JUNKET** / Pulverize the milk with the iota powder and salt. Bring to a boil and allow to cool to 34-36°C. Add the rennet and leave to set in a cool place. **CHEESE SAND** / Grate the cheese with a Microplane grater and mix it with the ground almonds. Roll the egg in the mixture and fry briefly at 200°C. **CHEESE LEAVES** / Pulverize the cheese with the oil. Use a round pastry cutter to form leaves. Just before serving, brush the leaves with the remaining cheese oil.

PLATING / Arrange the breaded egg with some junket, a blue cheese egg and a cheese leaf on a plate. Decorate with cheese sand and a seasoned milk crisp dusted with a pinch of baobab powder.

SQUID ON LEAVES

— Serves 4. —

SQUID

12 line-caught baby squid
Grated zest of ½ lemon
1 garlic clove, finely chopped
3 g rock tea
100 g olive oil
Salt and powdered ginger

SQUID SAUCE

1 onion
1 lemongrass stalk
200 g milk
3 tbsp extra virgin olive oil
Salt and pepper

ROCK TEA BALLS

100 g water
1 g rock tea
10 g sugar
1 g kappa carrageenan
150 g olive oil

RED PEPPER DROPS

100 g olive oil
20 g raw piquillo pepper
Salt and sugar

BLACK POTATO SLICES AND OIL

300 g olive oil
20 g freeze-dried squid ink
1 potato
Salt and pepper

OTHER INGREDIENTS

Kaffir lime leaves and pea sprouts

SQUID / Clean the squid thoroughly, separate and set the bodies aside. Reserve the ink, fins and tentacles for other recipes. Make two perpendicular cuts into the closed end of the squid. Make a marinade with the remaining ingredients and marinate the squid for 10 minutes. Set aside. **SQUID SAUCE** / Peel and julienne the onion. Cook it in boiling water with half a stalk of lemongrass. When the onion is tender, strain and remove the lemongrass. Place the other half of the lemongrass stalk in the milk and bring to a boil. Allow to infuse away from the heat for 5 minutes. Strain. Pulverize the cooked onion with the milk. Strain and season. Stir in the oil before serving. **ROCK TEA BALLS** / Boil all the ingredients except the oil. Use a dropper to drop the tea spheres into the oil one at a time. Reserve for later. **RED PEPPER DROPS** / Pulverize the peppers with the oil. Season with a little salt and sugar. **BLACK POTATO SLICES AND OIL**/ Mix the ink in 100 g oil until it has dissolved completely. Peel the potato and cut into thin rectangular slices. Season and confit in olive oil over low heat. When cooked through, remove the potato slices from the oil and brush with some black ink oil.

PLATING / Present the baby squid on a bed of kaffir lime leaves in a wooden box. Paint a brushstroke of black oil on a plate and beside it, place a slice of confit potato. Add some pea sprouts, red pepper drops and rock tea spheres. Accompany sparingly with the sauce. Once the plate has been placed in front of the diner, the squid on lime leaves is presented in the box and plated at the table.

EAT YOUR FRUIT AND VEG

— Serves 4. —

MELON

200 g melon
100 g melon liqueur
200 g simple syrup
1 vanilla bean

TOMATOES

100 g water
125 g sugar
30 g sherry vinegar
2 cloves
4 coriander seeds
12 cherry tomatoes

CHIA SHARDS

125 g fondant
65 g liquid glucose
65 g isomalt sugar
12 g chia seeds

LEMON SAUCE

100 g lemon juice
3 g sweet paprika
60 g sugar
0.5 g Xantana

OTHER INGREDIENTS

powdered sumac

ORANGE DROPS

75 g orange juice
75 g carrot juice
30 g sugar
35 g pure albumen (powdered egg whites)

LEMON MERINGUE

75 g sugar
30 g water
115 g egg white
Grated zest of 1 lemon
0.2 g lavender powder

MELON / Peel and clean the melon. Cut into four 5 x 2 cm rectangles. Pour the melon liqueur and the syrup into a bowl. Slit the vanilla bean open and add. Place the melon and the other ingredients in a vacuum bag. Vacuum seal and refrigerate for 2 hours. **TOMATOES** / Wash the tomatoes. Place the water, sugar, vinegar, cloves and coriander seeds in a saucepan and bring to a boil. Add the tomatoes and boil for approximately 3 minutes, depending on the size and ripeness. Remove from the water, peel and reserve. **CHIA SHARDS** / Heat the fondant, glucose and sugar to 160ºC in a saucepan. Cool to 140ºC and stir in the chia seeds. Spread small amounts of the mixture on a silicone mat to form small shards. **LEMON SAUCE** / Pulverize all the ingredients together in a food processor. Let the sauce settle to remove any air bubbles. Set aside. **ORANGE DROPS**/ Beat the orange juice, carrot juice, sugar and albumen into stiff peaks, as for a meringue. Once the mixture is stiff, drop it in tear-shaped drops onto a baking tray. Bake in the oven at 170°C for 5 minutes. Store in an airtight container. **LEMON MERINGUE** / Heat the water and sugar to 120ºC to make a syrup. Meanwhile, beat the egg whites until stiff. When the syrup has reached the right temperature, incorporate it in small amounts to the egg whites, whisking continuously. Add the grated lemon zest and lavender powder at the end. Set aside.

PLATING / To present the dish, arrange the melon slices on the plate. Dust the tomatoes lightly with the powdered sumac and lay a few on the melon. Place some lemon meringue next to it and add a few orange drops. Sauce sparingly.

SIZZLING SQUID

— Serves 4. —

SQUID

12 line-caught baby squid

SQUID MARINADE

The zest and juice of ½ lemon
50 g extra virgin olive oil
2 g soumbala powder
0.8 g white pepper
Sarsaparilla root
Salt and powdered ginger

SQUID INK SAUCE

1 onion
2 Italian green peppers
1 garlic clove
25 g olive oil
1 cuttlefish (300 g)
1 small tomato
½ glass red wine
Salt

MELON BALLS

½ muskmelon
100 g squid ink sauce
150 g beetroot juice

FRUIT BROTH

1000 g water
10 g fresh mint leaves
10 g fresh oregano leaves
5 g sycamore syrup
2 g cherry tea
Zest of ¼ lemon
1 g Xantana

HOT PLATE

500 g coarse sea salt
Pandan leaves

OTHER INGREDIENTS

2 cast-iron or stone plates

SQUID / Clean the squid thoroughly and separate the bodies. Save the ink, fins and tentacles for the sauce. Cut through the end of the squid. Set aside. **SQUID MARINADE** / Combine all the ingredients and leave the squid in the mixture for 2 minutes. Pan-fry the squid until golden in a drop of olive oil on a hot frying pan. **SQUID INK SAUCE** / Finely chop the onion, peppers and garlic and sauté gently in the olive oil. Clean the cuttlefish and add the ink to the ink from the squid. Cut the cuttlefish and squid into medium-sized pieces. When the vegetables are soft and translucent, add the squid and cuttlefish. Sauté together for 15 minutes. Add the chopped tomato and cook until soft. Add the wine and leave to reduce. Dilute the ink in water and add. Stir well and add enough extra water to cover the fish. Let simmer for about 30 minutes over medium heat. Remove the fish and pulverize the sauce ingredients in a food processor. Press through a sieve and season. **MELON BALLS** / Use a small melon scoop to scoop out the melon balls. Place half in a vacuum bag with the beetroot juice. Bag at 80% vacuum. Put the remaining balls into another vacuum bag with the lightly diluted squid ink sauce. Bag as for the first half. Leave the bags sealed for one hour. Open and set aside. **FRUIT BROTH** / Boil all the ingredients except the Xantana for 2 minutes. Strain and season with salt and pepper. Add the Xantana and mix with a hand-blender. Clarify the broth by eliminating bubbles in a vacuum sealer or let sit for 24 hours until clear. **BASE OF THE HOT PLATE** / Cut the leaves into 20cm lengths. Set aside.

PLATING / Arrange the coloured melon balls on a white plate, sauce lightly with the squid sauce. Cover the surface of a *very* hot stone or cast-iron plate with a layer of salt. Arrange the pandan leaves on the salt. Place the squid on top. Pour the hot broth around the squid at the dining table to produce a gush of steam and a pleasant aroma. At the table, plate the squid next to the melon balls.

The sensations of the smoked leaves produced at the last moment. Sweet and deep, but they only contribute smell, not taste. A perfect combination for one of the most delicate flavours: the one that comes from the baby squid.

— *Sizzling squid* —

RED CHILLI PEPPER VENISON

— Serves 4. —

MOJO SAUCE

100 g cooked black beans
2 tbsp sherry vinegar
Salt and pepper

VENISON

800 g rack of roe deer or other venison
Salt and pepper

SAUCE

500 g venison bones
1 garlic clove, julienned
2 onions, julienned
1 shallot, julienned
250 g water
250 g venison stock
Salt and black pepper

RED CHILLI PEPPERS

12 pickled guindilla chillies from Ibarra
125 g water
6 g vegetable gelling agent
0.2 g sweet paprika
2 g cochineal food colouring

TURMERIC DROPS

75 g cocoa butter
5 g turmeric
250 g liquid nitrogen

BRUSSELS SPROUT PETALS

2 Brussels sprouts
¼ garlic clove, chopped
3 tbsp olive oil
Water
Salt

BLACK BEANS

200 g black beans
½ spring onion
½ green pepper
2 tbsp olive oil
Water
Salt

SPINACH ROUNDS

4 spinach leaves
1 tbsp olive oil
Water
Salt

MOJO SAUCE / Mix all the ingredients and pulverize in a food processor. Season with salt and pepper. **VENISON** / Clean, trim, and portion the rack. Coat the pieces with the mojo sauce and brown well on both sides. Set aside. **SAUCE** / Lightly brown the bones with a drop of oil. Add the garlic, onions and shallot, and sauté for a few minutes. Remove excess fat, add the stock and water. Simmer for 2 hours. Strain and season with salt and pepper. Set aside. **RED CHILLI PEPPERS** / Pulverize all the ingredients in a food processor except the chilli peppers and bring to a boil. Hold the peppers by their stems and dip in the mixture. Set aside. **TURMERIC DROPS** / Melt the cocoa butter along with the turmeric in a saucepan. Add the mixture drop by drop to the liquid nitrogen. Remove the frozen drops and keep chilled until ready to use. **BRUSSELS SPROUT PETALS** / Separate the leaves and clean well. Blanch in boiling water with salt. Cool in ice water. Drain and add the garlic sautéed in olive oil. **BLACK BEANS** / Cook the beans together with chopped green pepper, spring onion, oil, salt and water to cover. Simmer in a casserole over low heat until the beans are soft. It is important that the beans remain whole. **SPINACH ROUNDS** / Clean the spinach leaves and remove any tough parts. Blanch in boiling water with salt. Cool in ice water. Drain and spread out. Use a cookie cutter to give them a round shape. Season lightly and paint with olive oil. Set aside.

PLATING / Place the venison fillets in the centre of the plate. Arrange the rest of the ingredients around the venison. Top with sauce.

CHOCOLATE AND COLOURED SHARDS

— Serves 4. —

PURPLE WAFER

165 g chopped red cabbage
200 g water
70 g sugar
3.5 g Xantana
Water (for blanching)

WHITE WAFER

200 g skimmed milk
70 g sugar
3 g Xantana
Ground, freeze-dried beetroot, parsley, and tomato powders

ORANGE WAFER

200 g pumpkin juice
2 g Xantana
20 g sugar

TONKA BEAN AND CARDAMOM MOUSSE

30 g cream
10 cardamom seeds
1 sheet gelatin (2 g)
200 g dark chocolate
30 g butter
4 egg yolks
½ tonka bean
4 egg whites
50 g sugar

GARLIC AND VANILLA COULIS

200 g water
Juice of ½ lemon
0.2 g Xantana
½ vanilla pod
50 g sugar
1 garlic clove

CHOCOLATE CROUTONS

100 g water
20 g sugar
20 g cocoa
1 slice of bread cut into small cubes

PURPLE WAFER / Bring 200 g water to the boil. Add 65 g of the chopped red cabbage and cook for 2 minutes. Strain and keep the cabbage for other uses. This recipe uses only the cooking water. Blanch the rest of the red cabbage in boiling water. Purée in a food processor. Reserve the cabbage purée (about 90 g). Pulverize the rest of the cabbage with 110 g of the cooking water, juice, sugar and the Xantana. Spread the mixture thinly on a silicone mat and dehydrate at 60ºC. Store in a dry place until ready to use. **WHITE WAFER** / Pulverize the milk, sugar and Xantana in a food processor. Spread the mixture in a thin layer on a silicone mat and sprinkle with the freeze-dried powders. Dehydrate at 60ºC. Store in a dry place until ready to use. **ORANGE WAFER** / Pulverize all the ingredients in a food processor. Spread the mixture in a thin layer on a silicone mat and dehydrate at 60ºC. Store in a dry place until ready to use. **TONKA BEAN AND CARDAMOM MOUSSE** / Boil the cream with the cardamom seeds and the presoaked gelatin. Allow the cream to infuse until ready to use. Melt the chocolate and butter together and allow to cool. Add the yolks, cream and grated tonka bean to the chocolate and butter and mix thoroughly. Gently fold in the stiffly beaten egg whites and sugar. Refrigerate the mousse for 3 hours. Smoke the chocolate mousse for 5 minutes in a smoker. **GARLIC AND VANILLA COULIS** / Pulverize the water, lemon juice and Xantana in a food processor. Place the mixture in a vacuum bag and seal. Cook sous-vide for 2 hours at 65ºC. **CHOCOLATE CROUTONS** / Boil the water, sugar and cocoa together and pour the mixture over the bread cubes. Dehydrate at 65ºC until completely dry.

PLATING / Arrange small spoonfuls of mousse and coloured crisps on the plate. Add some vanilla and garlic cream and chocolate croutons.

LOBSTER CORALINE

— Serves 4. —

ROASTED ONIONS

2 onions, peeled and halved
2 g cochineal food colouring
150 g cola liquor
20 g olive oil

ONION FILLING

25 g poached onion
15 g diced mango
Lobster tomalley
2 tbsp white wine
Pinch of cinnamon and nutmeg.
1 tbsp olive oil
Salt and pepper

GREEN CLAY

50 g water
10 g blanched spinach
3 g freeze-dried barley grass
15 g sugar
100 g olive oil
30 g clay
A few drops of lemon
Salt and pepper

CHILLI PEPPER MOJO SAUCE

100 g olive oil
100 g pickled guindilla chillies
20 g toasted bread
1 garlic clove, fried
15 g sugar
Salt and pepper

LOBSTER

2 lobsters (350 g each)
Salt, ginger and liquorice powder

CORAL CRISP

140 g water
110 g flour
30 g Trisol (soluble fibre derived from wheat)
1 g cochineal food colouring
25 g flax seeds
Olive oil for frying

OTHER INGREDIENTS

Nori seaweed powder

LOBSTER / Split the lobster in half and separate the body and claws from the head. Save the heads for making broths or sauces. Thread two wooden skewers through the tails to keep them straight when blanched. Plunge into an ice bath. Peel and portion. Season and sprinkle with liquorice and ginger. Set aside. **GREEN CLAY** / Pulverize all the ingredients until they form a very creamy green paste. Season with salt and pepper. **CHILLI PEPPER MOJO SAUCE** / Pulverize all the ingredients in a food processor. Season with salt and pepper. **ROASTED ONIONS** / Place onions, cochineal colouring, cola and olive oil on a baking sheet. Season with salt and pepper and bake for 60 minutes at 140ºC. Separate the onion layers and cut the larger ones in half. **ONION FILLING** / Lightly sauté the onion, mango and tomalley from the heads of the lobsters in oil. Add the wine and the rest of the ingredients. Season with salt and pepper. **CORAL CRISP** / Combine all the ingredients except the flax seeds in a bowl and mix well. Cut some rectangular sheets of oven paper. Spread each sheet with the flour, Trisol and water preparation. Sprinkle flax seeds on top. Heat the oil to 190ºC and fry lightly. Drain well and remove the paper from the crisp.

PLATING / Cut the lobster tail into pieces and lightly spread with the chilli pepper mojo sauce. Sauté on both sides in a frying pan with a drop of oil. Finish cooking the body and the claws in the salamander. Spread the green clay on the plate using a small spatula and set the onion slices on top. Place the filling on the onion and the lobster on top. Accompany with the coral crisp. Sprinkle with a pinch of nori seaweed powder.

OYSTERS WITH HAM AND CITRUS

— *Serves 4.* —

OYSTERS

12 oysters
Powdered ginger

TRUFFLE VINAIGRETTE

45 g peanut oil
7 g sherry vinegar
12.5 g jus de truffe
2.5 g salt

SEAWEED

200 g kombu in brine
2 tbsp olive oil

CHAMPAGNE SAUCE

200 g champagne
20 g sugar
3 g chopped pickled ginger

CITRUS FRUIT

1 orange
1 grapefruit
1 tangerine

OTHER INGREDIENTS

a pinch of chopped fried oyster, slices of cured ham, chopped chives, fried canary grass seeds and toasted potato flakes

---

OYSTERS / Open the oysters and set them aside in their own juice. **TRUFFLE VINIAGRETTE** / Combine all the ingredients. **SEAWEED** / Desalt the seaweed and julienne. Remove excess water with a cloth. Heat the oil and sauté lightly. Set aside. **CHAMPAGNE SAUCE** / Combine all the ingredients and half of the champagne in a blender and pulverize. Then stir in the other half. Set aside. **CITRUS FRUIT** / Use a paring knife to peel and remove the pith from the citrus, and then cut each segment out. Remove the pith from half the orange peel and chop up the zest. Store in cold water and set aside. Keep the citrus segments and some of the cold champagne sauce until ready to use.

PLATING / Cover the bottom of a wooden box with the sautéed seaweed. Warm the oysters with some truffle vinaigrette under the grill. Place them on top of the seaweed. Arrange the rest of the ingredients in a soup plate. Add the warmed dressing at the last minute. The oysters are then added to the plate at the table.

Citrus fruits are great allies for the gustatory force of an oyster. If we play with the range they offer us, delving deeper in the acid and the bitter, it produces a very powerful dish.

—— Oysters with ham and citrus ——

BLOOD-RED APPLE

— Serves 4. —

FOIE GRAS PASTE

200 g fresh foie gras
55 g cream cheese
45 g kéfir
1 tbsp extra virgin olive oil
Salt, black pepper, powdered ginger and liquorice root

COLD FOIE GRAS COATING

25 g ground almonds
25 g chopped pistachios
25 g dried grated coconut
1.5 g dehydrated white hibiscus flower

BLOOD APPLE

1 reinette apple
25 g beetroot juice

'MOTHER-OF-PEARL' POTATO

1 potato
0.5 g edible silver powder
Salt

SAUCE

0.6 g water
½ leek
50 g potato
50 g light cream
Salt and pepper

OTHER INGREDIENTS

Vananco leaves and chilli threads

FOIE GRAS PASTE / Cut the foie gras into cubes and pan-fry. Allow to sit for 5 minutes and pulverize together with the cheese, kéfir and oil. Season the mixture and add some ground ginger and liquorice root. Set aside. Pour into half sphere silicone moulds and let set in the refrigerator. Remove the foie gras spheres from the mould and set aside. **COLD FOIE GRAS COATING** / Combine all the ingredients well. Form the balls by pressing two half spheres together. Then roll in the coating. **BLOOD APPLE** / Use a hypodermic needle to prick over the apple in several places. Place the apple in a vacuum bag with the beetroot juice. Bag at 100% vacuum and keep sealed for 5 minutes. Remove the apple and cut it into thin slices with a meat slicer or mandolin. Set aside. **'MOTHER,-OF-PEARL' POTATO** / Cook the potato in boiling water with a pinch of salt. Drain well and peel. Pulverize with the silver powder and season. Spread the mixture out very thinly on a sheet of greaseproof paper and dehydrate at 55°C. Remove from the paper and cut into irregular rectangles. Fry lightly at 150°C and drain. Set aside. **SAUCE** / Wash, peel, and chop the leek and potato. Simmer in water over low heat. When the potato is cooked, strain and pulverize the ingredients in a food processor with the cream. Season with salt and pepper.

PLATING / Heat the apple slices briefly under the grill. Arrange the coated foie gras on a plate, and cover with the apple. Drizzle lightly with the sauce and decorate with the chilli threads, 'mother-of-pearl' potato and a few Vananco leaves.

DUCK
AND BIRDSEED

— Serves 4. —

MOJO SAUCE

50 g blueberry purée
50 g almond purée
Salt and pepper

DUCK

2 wild duck, cleaned
Salt, ginger and liquorice powder

SAUCE

2 duck carcasses
3 medium onions
4 leeks
1 pinch fresh thyme
1 pinch citronella
200 g olive oil
Duck fat from the carcass
Salt and pepper

PUMPKIN SEEDS

50 g pumpkin seeds, shelled
65 g water
0.25 g Xantana
Salt and black pepper

GRAPESEED EMULSION

50 g grapeseed flour
75 g water
5 g white wine vinegar
25 g sugar
15 g brown sugar
75 g olive oil
Salt and pepper

SUNFLOWER SEEDS

100 g orange juice
10 g sugar
50 g sunflower seeds, shelled and fried

MOJO SAUCE / Pulverize all of the ingredients in a blender to form a thick paste. Season and set aside. **DUCK** / Remove the breasts from the duck and season them lightly. Spread the breasts with the mojo and cook them on the grill. Set aside. Use the carcasses and rest of the parts for the sauce. **SAUCE** / Cut up the carcasses and brown them in a pan with a little oil. Chop the vegetables and use the remaining oil to brown lightly in the rest of the oil. Strain the vegetables, add to the carcasses and sauté together with the thyme. Cover with water and allow to reduce. Strain and season. Add a few drops of oil and a pinch of citronella. **PUMPKIN SEEDS** / Pulverize the pumpkin seeds and water. Strain and season. Add the Xantana, making sure it dissolves completely. **GRAPESEED EMULSION** / Combine all the ingredients except the oil, salt and pepper, and mix well. Add the oil and emulsify the mixture. Season with salt and pepper. **SUNFLOWER SEEDS** / Make a light brown caramel with the sugar and orange juice. Remove from heat and let cool slightly. Add the sunflower seeds and mix together. Set aside in a cool, dry place.

PLATING / Cut the duck breast into pieces. Plate a piece of duck beside a mound of sunflower seeds. Garnish the plate with the other seed mixtures and sauce.

REEF(ER) LOBSTER WITH HEMP SEED MUSTARD

— *Serves 4.* —

LOBSTER

2 lobsters (350 g each)
Salt, powdered ginger and liquorice root

HEMP SEED MOJO SAUCE

50 g olive oil
50 g toasted almonds
50 g whole grain mustard
25 g hemp seeds
2 tbsp water
Salt and pepper

SWEET PAPRIKA OIL

100 g olive oil
10 g sweet paprika

HEMP SEED EMULSION

1 egg
½ litre olive oil (0.4%)
1 tbsp turmeric
15 g toasted hemp seeds
Salt and pepper

'PINCERS'

2 onions
1 leek
1 carrot
50 g olive oil
2 lobster heads
100 g red vermouth
2 g vegetable gelling agent
A clothespin silicone mould
Salt, sugar and powdered ginger

HEMP SEED CRACKERS

110 g water
120 g flour
30 g Trisol (soluble wheat fibre)
1 g turmeric
25 g hemp seeds
Olive oil for frying

HEMP SEED OIL

200 g olive oil (0.4%)
40 g hemp seeds

OTHER INGREDIENTS

Syrha leaves

LOBSTER / Cut the lobster in half and separate the body and claws from the head. Save the heads for the 'pincers' mixture. Push two skewers through the body to prevent it from curling when blanched. Blanch the body in boiling water and cool it down quickly afterwards by submerging it in a bowl of iced water. Peel and cut into even-sized portions. Season and sprinkle with some ground ginger and liquorice root. Set aside. **HEMP SEED MOJO SAUCE** / Pulverize all the ingredients together. Season with salt and pepper. **SWEET PAPRIKA OIL** / Heat the oil and paprika together for five minutes at 55ºC. Allow to settle before using. **HEMP SEED OIL** / Pulverize the oil and seeds and allow to settle. Set aside. **HEMP SEED EMULSION** / Emulsify the egg and oil as if you were making mayonnaise. Add the rest of the ingredients. Season with salt and pepper. **'PINCERS'** / Peel and chop the vegetables and sauté in oil in a pan. When they are soft and translucent, add the lobster heads and cook together for a few minutes. Add the vermouth and cover with water. Allow to simmer for one hour. Remove the heads and pulverize them in a blender. Strain through a chinois, season and add the gelling agent (2 g gelling agent to 200 g of sauce). Bring back to a boil. Pour the mixture into the silicone moulds and leave to set. Unmould the clothespin 'pincers' and set aside. **HEMP SEED CRACKERS** / Mix the flour, turmeric, Trisol and water together in a bowl. Cut some greaseproof paper into rectangular pieces. Coat each rectangle with the mixture. Sprinkle the hemp seeds over the top. Heat the oil to 190ºC and fry the crackers (with the paper) until lightly golden. Drain well and remove the paper. **PLATING** / Cut the lobster into pieces and dip it lightly into the mojo sauce. Pan-fry quickly on both sides with a drop of oil. Finish cooking the body and claws under the grill. Arrange the lobster on the plate, to one side sparingly add some emulsion and some Syrha leaves, lightly dressed with some hemp seed oil. Drizzle over some paprika oil and arrange the crackers and the 'pincers' carefully to complete the dish.

WHITE TUNA
AND CINNAMON

— *Serves 4.* —

MOJO SAUCE

2 g cinnamon powder
100 g toasted bread
40 g olive oil
Juice of 1 lemon
1 onion, boiled
Salt and pepper

TUNA BELLY

400 g white tuna belly, cleaned with skin on
Salt
Ginger

CHOPPED NUTS

5 g millet
2 g nori powder
5 g pine nuts
5 g pistachios
2 g chia seeds
2 g canary grass
10 marcona almonds
Zest from ½ an orange
Salt

CINNAMON STICKS

4 cinnamon sticks
100 g oil
1 g cinnamon powder

SAUCE

100 g orange juice
40 g soy sauce
20 g lemon juice
1 g cinnamon powder

OTHER INGREDIENTS

4 glass bell jars

MOJO SAUCE / Pulverize all ingredients together. Season with salt, pepper and a touch of sugar. **TUNA BELLY** / Portion the tuna belly into rectangles, 2 per serving (one should be slightly larger than the other). Season with salt and a pinch of ginger. Sear the tuna with a bit of oil on the skin-side only. Remove the skin, brush with a bit of the mojo sauce and finish in the salamander. Set aside. **CHOPPED NUTS** / Bake each type of nut or seed separately. Allow to cool, chop the nuts and mix together, adding the orange zest and salt. Set aside. **CINNAMON STICKS** / Mix the cinnamon powder and the oil. Soak the cinnamon sticks in the oil until ready to use. **SAUCE** / Combine the ingredients except the cinnamon and boil for 1 minute. Add the cinnamon and allow to sit.

PLATING / Stand the tuna rectangles upright in the centre of the plate. Place the cinnamon stick to one side, light it and then blow out the flame. Cover the dish with the bell jar. The stick will continue smoking, lending the fish a slightly smoky flavour. Remove the bell jar in front of the guest.

It's fun to associate the astringent sensations that cinnamon usually gives us – although not always – linked to the sweet world, and transfer them to the salty world. They produce different sensations. Even more so if you use it as incense.

—— *White tuna and cinnamon* ——

SOLE IN CANE

— *Serves 4.* —

SOLES

2 soles (500 g each)
Salt
Ginger powder
Olive oil 0,4°

SUGAR CANE

4 pieces of cane (10 cm each)

MOJO

100 g cooked chickpeas
30 g cooked spinach
20 g olive oil
1 sprig fresh dill
Salt and pepper

ORANGE SAUCE

100 g blended carrot
100 g orange juice
1 g turmeric powder
1 g xanthan gum
Salt and pepper

CUPUAZÚ SAUCE

100 g virgin olive oil
2 g cupuazú
10 g icing sugar
10 g chopped parsley
10 g chopped dried ham
Salt and pepper

SOLES / Sprinkle the soles with salt and ginger. Grease them with oil and grill them. Before they are ready, fillet them, cover them slightly with the mojo and finish the cooking on the salamander. **MOJO** / Mix all the ingredients and blend them. Adjust the seasoning if necessary. **SUGAR CANE** / Strain the canes and cut them vertically. Remove all the 'flesh' and cut them into sticks. Set aside. **ORANGE SAUCE** / Combine the carrot, the turmeric, the orange and the xanthan gum in a pan. Blend the mixture, then boil it and season with salt and pepper. Set aside. **CUPUAZÚ SAUCE** / Mix the ingredients and season them with salt and pepper.

PLATING / Set half a cane on a plate, painting its interior with the mojo. Put the sole on the top of the cane and cover it with the remaining half cane. Slightly warm up the dish. Finish the serving by adding the orange sauce in the form of drops and also its own mojo in the same way. Place the cane sticks on one side. Pour the cupuazú sauce over the plate in front of the guest.

217

SOY DUCK

— Serves 4. —

MOJO SAUCE

100 g cooked black soy beans
50 g soy sauce
30 g orange juice
Salt and pepper
Powdered ginger

WILD DUCK

2 wild ducks
Salt, powdered ginger and liquorice root

SAUCE

2 duck carcasses
3 medium onions
4 leeks
1 bouquet garni
200 g olive oil
Chopped chives
Oil from the sautéed duck bones
Salt and pepper

WHITE SOY BEANS

100 g white soy beans
10 g leek
10 g carrot
Water
Olive oil for frying
Salt

GREEN SPROUTS

30 g mung beans
Water

BLACK SOY BEANS

50 g black soy beans
Water

TOFU

100 g fresh tofu
Pinch of powdered cinnamon
Pinch of confectioner's sugar
Pinch of oregano
Pinch of thyme
Pinch of basil

SOY VINAIGRETTE

50 g olive oil
10 g sherry vinegar
5 g honey
1 g paprika
Salt and pepper

MOJO SAUCE / Pulverize all the ingredients to make a thick paste. Season with salt, pepper and a hint of ginger. Set aside. **WILD DUCK** / Remove the duck breasts and season lightly. Generously coat the breasts with the mojo and cook on a flat top grill. Set aside. Save the carcasses and other parts for the sauce. **SAUCE** / Cut up the carcasses and brown them in a pan with a little oil. Chop the vegetables and sauté in a separate pan in the remaining oil until golden. Strain the vegetables, add to the carcasses and sauté well. Cover with water and allow the sauce to reduce. Strain and season. Add a few drops of oil and the chopped chives at the end. **WHITE SOY BEANS** / Cover the beans in water and soak for 6 hours. Boil the beans in water with the leek, carrot and a pinch of salt. Once cooked, drain well and cool. Heat the oil and fry the beans in small batches. Season. **GREEN SPROUTS** / Cover the beans in water and soak for 6 hours. Place in a damp cotton cloth and moisten every 6 hours until they sprout. The process can take up to 4 or 5 days. Use the whole sprout. **BLACK SOY BEANS** / Cover the beans in water and soak for 6 hours. **TOFU** / Cut the tofu into 1 cm-square cubes. Sprinkle half the cubes with equal parts sugar and cinnamon. Sprinkle the rest with equal parts of the remaining three ingredients. **SOY VINAIGRETTE** / Combine all the ingredients, season and set aside.

PLATING / Place the sliced duck breast on the plate. Arrange the accompanying ingredients separately around it.

OYSTERS MONDRIAN

— Serves 4. —

OYSTERS

12 oysters

GREEN MOJO SAUCE

100 g olive oil
1 roasted onion
6 mizuna leaves
30 g runner beans, fried
10 g dried apricots, cooked
1 garlic clove, fried
30 g toasted almonds
30 g blanched courgette peel
Salt and pepper

MACA SAUCE

4 g black maca
60 g olive oil
10 g sherry vinegar
20 g courgette, diced
Salt and pepper

MONDRIAN

25 g confectioner's sugar
20 g sugar
120 g flour
½ egg
35 g butter
120 g passion fruit pulp
Salt
5 g spirulina powder
5 g cochineal food colouring
2 g charred aubergine powder

TRUFFLE VINAIGRETTE

90 g peanut oil
14 g sherry vinegar
25 g truffle juice
5 g salt

OTHER INGREDIENTS

fried pumpkin seeds, sautéed pumpkin balls, mini red-ribbon sorrel leaves and radish shoots.

OYSTERS / Open the oysters and set aside in their juice. **GREEN MOJO SAUCE** / Pulverize all ingredients together. Season with salt and pepper. **MACA SAUCE** / Mix all ingredients together, adding the diced courgette at the end. Season with salt and pepper. **MONDRIAN** / Mix all ingredients together, except the spirulina and cochineal food colouring. Pour 2 tablespoons of the batter on a waffle-cone maker and cook until lightly golden on both sides. Cut the wafer into squares and sprinkle with the different coloured powders.

PLATING / Brush the oysters with a little green mojo sauce and cook them gently in a pan. Lightly dress the oysters with the vinaigrette and lay them on a spoonful of the green marinade. Sauce and plate the rest of the ingredients, balancing the Mondrians over the oysters.

STOMPED FRUIT

— Serves 4. —

SHOELACES

60 g simple syrup
10 g liquid glucose
30 g cocoa powder
Pinch of silver powder

MOLE AND APRICOT PUDDING

75 g sugar (candy)
390 g apricot purée
60 g black mole sauce
4 eggs
100 g sugar
20 g brandy

SPICED SUGAR

60 g sugar
1 g dried thyme
1 g powdered liquorice
1 g powdered ginger
1 g powdered black pepper
1 g powdered dried parsley

FOOTPRINT

150 g ground almonds
1 egg white
150 g icing sugar
2 g squid ink
Boot-tread stencil
Pinch of gold powder

FRUIT*

½ mango
1 orange
50 g fresh peeled coconut
½ apple
60 g peeled pineapple
4 strawberries
1 peach
**Any seasonal fruit can be used*

SHOELACES / Mix all ingredients together, except the silver powder. Chill for 24 hours. Put the mixture in a piping bag and squeeze shoelace-sized lines on a silicone mat. Bake for 2 hours at 200ºC. Remove from oven and sprinkle with silver powder. **MOLE AND APRICOT PUDDING** / Caramelize 75 g of sugar and pour into rectangular silicone moulds. Pulverize the rest of the ingredients and pour into the moulds. Cook for 70 minutes at 100ºC. **SPICED SUGAR** / Mix all ingredients together and set aside. **FRUIT** / Clean, peel and cut into small pieces. Sprinkle the fruit with the spiced sugar. Place in a metal strainer and gently cook the fruit over a charcoal grill. **FOOTPRINT** / Mix the almonds together with the sugar, egg white and squid ink. Roll out the dough, giving it an irregular shape. Using a sheet of food-safe acetate, cut the dough into a footprint shape. Lay the boot-tread stencil on the black dough and sprinkle with gold powder. Bake for 8 minutes at 160ºC.

PLATING / On a dish that represents the pattern of a pavement (as on p. 223) , plate the pudding and fruit. Cover with the footprint and place the shoelaces to one side.

Our restaurant is a very urban place, and this is where part of the mystery lies. The pavement is a part of our identity. Playing with it can even help compose a dish. The footprint that remains, who steps on to leave its mark.

— *Stomped fruit* —

LOBSTER AND BEE POLLEN

— Serves 4. —

LOBSTER

2 lobsters (350 g each)
Salt, ginger and liquorice powder

POLLEN MOJO SAUCE

20 g dried pollen
20 g crusty bread
50 g tomato
1 garlic clove, fried
50 g almonds
50 g cola drink
Juice of ½ lemon
20 g freeze-dried potato purée
Salt and pepper

PICKLED VEGETABLES

1 broccoli stalk
100 g white wine vinegar
Salt and pepper

POTATO SAUCE

10 g kithul palm pulp
20 g orange juice
100 g olive oil
Salt and pepper

LOBSTER SAUCE

10 g kithul palm pulp
20 g orange juice
10 g black quinoa
Salt and pepper

POTATO HONEYCOMB

2 blue potatoes
50 g olive oil
Salt, pepper and ginger powder

OTHER INGREDIENTS

Fresh pollen, tender shoots

LOBSTER / Split the lobster in half and separate the tail and claws from the head. Save the heads for other recipes. Hold the lobster tail with two wooden skewers. Blanche the tail in boiling water and plunge into cold water. Peel and portion. Season and sprinkle with liquorice and ginger. Set aside. **POLLEN MOJO SAUCE** / Pulverize all the ingredients in a food processor. Season with salt and pepper. **PICKLED VEGETABLES** / Use a peeler to thinly slice the broccoli stalks. Soak in vinegar for 25 minutes. Drain and season with salt and pepper. **POTATO SAUCE** / Mix the ingredients together. Season with salt and pepper. **LOBSTER SAUCE** / Mix all the ingredients, adding the quinoa at the last minute. Season with salt and pepper. **POTATO HONEYCOMB** / Wrap the potatoes in plastic wrap and cook in the microwave. Peel and purée. Add the olive oil. Season with salt, pepper and ginger.

PLATING / Cut the lobster into pieces and coat it lightly with the mojo sauce. Sauté quickly with a drop of olive oil. Finish cooking the body and claws in the salamander. Plate and sauce the lobster. Arrange the broccoli stalks. Set the honeycomb template on the side of the plate and spread a thin layer of the potato purée on top. Remove template. Sprinkle the pollen around the plate along with the tender shoots.

WHITE TUNA
WITH GARLIC PETALS

— Serves 4. —

GUINDILLA CHILLI PEPPER MOJO SAUCE

10 pickled guindilla chilli peppers
200 g water
50 g toasted pine nuts
50 g olive oil (0.4%)
5 g soy sauce
Salt and sugar

TUNA BELLY

600 g white tuna (150 g/piece)
Salt and ginger powder

RED SAUCE

1 spring onion
2 green peppers
3 roasted piquillo peppers
2 garlic cloves
2 tbsp olive oil (0.4%)
4 strawberries
1 tbsp sherry vinegar
Salt and pepper

KAMUT

10 g kamut
Water
100 g olive oil (0.4%)
Salt

GARLIC PETALS

9 garlic cloves
900 g water
8 g freeze-dried red cabbage
6 g cochineal food colouring
8 g freeze-dried barley grass
75 g sugar

OTHER INGREDIENTS

2 tbsp grapeseed oil

GUINDILLA CHILLI PEPPER MOJO SAUCE / Pulverize the water and peppers in a food processor and strain. Save 40 g of the strained pulp and add 85 g of the liquid. Add the remaining ingredients and pulverize. Strain the mixture. Season with salt and a pinch of sugar. **TUNA BELLY** / Cut the tuna belly into rectangles (2 per piece). One of the rectangles should be slightly larger than the other. Lightly smoke the tuna for 4 minutes in the smoker. Season with salt and ginger, spread with mojo sauce and grill quickly on a flat top grill or in a frying pan making sure the fish stays moist. **RED SAUCE** / Clean the vegetables and roast them in the oven with oil at 175°C for 20 minutes. Add the strawberries and bake for 5 more minutes. Pulverize in a food processor and strain. Add the vinegar and season with salt and pepper. **GARLIC PETALS** / Peel the garlic and slice thinly with a mandolin. Blanch the slices in two changes of boiling water. Divide the water and sugar into three saucepans and add the red cabbage to one, the cochineal to another and the barley grass to the third. Bring all three pots to a boil. Divide the garlic among the three saucepans and cook for 2 minutes. Strain the garlic and spread individually on a sheet of oven paper. Dry at 55°C. Once dry, remove the garlic slices. Set each colour aside separately. **KAMUT** / Cook the kamut in boiling water with salt. Once cooked, spread on a tray with oven paper and let dry. Once dry, fry in hot oil. Season with salt.

PLATING / Stand the tuna pieces upright on the plate. On one side, place the colourful garlic previously seasoned with the oil and the fried kamut. Accompany with the sauce.

SQUAB WITH POTATO FEATHERS

— Serves 4. —

GREEN MOJO SAUCE

100 g ground toasted almonds
100 g olive oil
50 g lemon juice
30 g spinach, cooked and drained
1 garlic clove, fried
Salt and pepper

SQUAB

2 squabs, cleaned
Salt, powdered ginger and liquorice

PURPLE POTATOES

4 purple potatoes
20 g skimmed milk

SAUCE

2 squab carcasses
3 medium onions
4 leeks
Pinch of fresh thyme
200 g olive oil
Fat rendered from the squab bones
10 g dried apricots
10 g pineapple pulp
5 g capers in vinegar, drained
Salt and pepper

GREEN POTATOES

2 large potatoes
1 g spirulina powder
20 g water

RED POTATOES

2 large potatoes
1 g cochineal food colouring
20 g water

AROMATIC OIL

100 g olive oil (0.4%)
8 oregano leaves
1 garlic clove
8 tarragon leaves
4 thyme sprigs

GREEN MOJO SAUCE / Pulverize all ingredients together to form a thick paste. Season to taste. Set aside. **SQUAB** / Remove the breasts and season lightly. Spread with a thick layer of the green mojo sauce and grill. Set aside. Save the carcasses for the sauce. **SAUCE** / Cut up the carcasses and brown them in a pan with a bit of oil. Chop the vegetables and brown lightly in the rest of the oil. Drain the oil from the vegetables and add them to the browned carcasses. Sauté together with the thyme. Cover with water, reduce, strain, and season. Add a few drops of oil and the rest of the ingredients at the last minute. **PURPLE POTATOES** / Steam the potatoes until soft. Peel and purée. Add hot milk to 175 g of the puréed potatoes. Mix well and pass through a sieve. Using a spatula, spread the potato on oven paper in the shape of a thick comb. Dry at 60ºC. Set aside in a dry place. **GREEN POTATOES** / Steam the potatoes until soft. Peel and purée. Add warm water and the spirulina to 175 g of the puréed potatoes. Mix well. Using a spatula, spread the potato on oven paper in the shape of a thick comb. Dry at 60ºC. Set aside in a dry place. **RED POTATOES** / Steam the potatoes until soft. Peel and purée. Add warm water and the cochineal colouring to 175 g of the puréed potatoes. Mix well. Using a spatula, spread the potato on oven paper in the shape of a thick comb. Dry at 60ºC. Set aside in a dry place. **AROMATIC OIL** / Mix all the ingredients in a saucepan and let them confit at 100ºC for 4 hours. Only the oil will be used in the final dish.

PLATING / Paint a few brushstrokes of the green marinade on the plate and arrange the squab breasts on top. Dress the breasts with a bit of the aromatic oil and salt. Create a bouquet with the broken potato 'feathers' and set it on top. Sauce just before serving.

THE KOBE'S BEER

— Serves 4. —

BEEF

400 g wagyu beef

SAUCE

120 g onion broth
7 g sugar
15 g white miso
0.3 g Xantana
100 g dark beer
Salt and pepper

LEEK CAKE

3 eggs
30 g sugar
7 g freeze-dried leek powder
35 g flour

RED ONIONS

10 g vinegar from the pickled onions
5 g sugar
100 g beetroot juice
12 pickled spring onions
Salt

PEPPER-GRINDER SMOKE

2 tbsp dry ice
2 tbsp green tea powder

POMEGRANATE

½ pomegranate
½ tbsp olive oil
Salt

OTHER INGREDIENTS

1 stick of liquorice root

BEEF / Portion the meat, and season with salt and pepper. Temper for 30 minutes before use. **SAUCE** / Mix the broth, the sugar, white miso, and the Xantana. Pulverize together. Cook over low heat for 5 minutes. Add the beer and let cook another 5 minutes. Season. **LEEK CAKE** / Whip the eggs and sugar together until soft peaks form. Carefully fold in the freeze-dried leek and the flour, taking care not to deflate the batter. Bake at 180°C for 16 minutes in a cake mould. Let cool and cut into 5 x 2 cm rectangles. Lightly toast on the flat top grill with a drop of oil. **RED ONIONS** / Combine the vinegar and sugar in a saucepan and reduce by half. Add the beetroot juice and let simmer. Remove the outer layer of the onions and add to the liquid. Cook for 5 minutes more and season lightly. **PEPPER-GRINDER SMOKE** / Just before serving, put the dry ice and tea powder into a pepper grinder. **POME-GRANATE** / De-seed the pomegranate and sauté the seeds in oil. Season lightly with salt and pepper.

PLATING / Lightly grill the meat on a flat top grill. Garnish with the red onions, the pomegranate, the stick of liquorice and the leek cake. Sauce lightly. The server will 'smoke' the dish at the table by grinding the dry ice and tea powder over the beef.

Where performance, taste, the bitterness of beer and the counterpoint of the fat of the meat come together. In the middle, the cold shower of rain through a pepper shaker that pours iced tea.

— *The kobe's beer* —

SPACE EGG

— Serves 4. —

EGG
4 eggs (60 g each)
Salt

RED COLOUR
1 can piquillo peppers (330 g)
1 g annatto
Salt and sugar

YELLOW TURMERIC
100 g chicken broth
3 g turmeric
1 g Xantana

SPINACH AND PARSLEY PURÉE
50 g parsley leaves
100 g spinach leaves
2 teaspoons olive oil
Salt

PIG'S FEET
2 pig's feet (halved and cleaned)
1 leek
1 carrot
1 onion
70 g panko bread crumbs
Water
Olive oil for frying
Salt

ST. GEORGE'S MUSHROOMS
90 g St. George's mushrooms
Olive oil (0.4%)
Pinch of parsley
Salt and black pepper

PUMPKIN BALLS
100 g pumpkin
1 tsp olive oil
1 tsp sherry vinegar
Salt and pepper

EGG / Boil the eggs for 40 minutes at 63ºC. Let sit for a minute. Carefully remove the shells and place the eggs on a plate. Season and set aside. **RED COLOUR** / Pulverize the peppers in a blender. Season with salt and sugar. Set 2 tablespoons of purée aside. Spread the mixture thinly between two sheets of oven paper and dehydrate at 60ºC. Once dry, cut the sheets just big enough to cover the egg. Add the annatto to the 2 tablespoons of piquillo purée and pulverize again. **YELLOW TUMERIC** / Boil the broth. Remove from heat and add the turmeric and Xantana. Pulverize and let sit. **SPINACH AND PARSLEY PURÉE** / Boil the parsley leaves in abundant salted water. When soft, remove and chill quickly in ice water. Drain well. Repeat the same process with the spinach leaves. Mix the parsley and spinach with the oil and purée, adding a bit of water as needed to make a green paste. **PIG'S FEET** / Put the pig's feet, leek, carrot and onion into a pressure cooker. Season and cook for 60 minutes once the pressure indicator has risen. Set the broth and vegetables aside and debone the trotters. Place one trotter on top of the other in a rectangular mould. Let cool. Cut into small cubes and dredge in panko crumbs. Fry in olive oil. Drain well on kitchen paper and season to taste. **ST. GEORGE'S MUSHROOMS** / Clean and halve the mushrooms. Lightly sauté half of the mushrooms with a drop of olive oil. Season all of them. **PUMPKIN BALLS** / Carve out balls of pumpkin with a melon baller. Sauté in the oil. Add the vinegar, salt and pepper at the last minute.

PLATING / Plate the egg and the mushrooms in a shallow bowl and cover with a strip of red pepper. Arrange the pumpkin balls around the egg and dot the dish with the green, yellow and red mixtures.

CHARCOAL-GRILLED OYSTERS

— Serves 4. —

OYSTERS

8 oysters

LEEK

1 leek
100 g butter
Salt and pepper

GREEN MOJO SAUCE

50 g pistachio paste
20 g toasted bread
30 g oyster sauce
30 g soy and yuzu sauce
200 g ground almonds
1 charred flour tortilla
30 g honey
Zest from ½ lemon
Salt and pepper

BLACK GARLIC PURÉE

75 g black garlic
20 g chicken broth
Salt and pepper

CHARCOAL OIL

150 g olive oil
A small piece of charcoal

SESAME BRUSHSTROKES

80 g black sesame paste
20 g chicken broth

OTHER INGREDIENTS

Mint leaves, fried walnuts and a few
drops of lemon juice

OYSTERS / Open the oysters and set them aside in their own juice. Clean the oyster shells and set them aside. **LEEK** / Clean and finely julienne the leek. Sauté in butter but do not brown. Season with salt and pepper. **GREEN MOJO SAUCE** / Pulverize all the ingredients in a food processor. Season with salt and pepper. **BLACK GARLIC PURÉE** / Mix the garlic with the broth and pulverize in a food processor. Strain. Season with salt and pepper. **CHARCOAL OIL** / Add the charcoal to the oil and let sit for 10 minutes. Strain and set aside. **SESAME BRUSHSTROKES** / Dilute the paste with the broth.

PLATING / Put a bit of sautéed leek in the bottom part of the oyster shell. Place the oyster on the leek and add a bit of juice. Paint a circle around the oyster using some of the green mojo sauce. Finish by adding a few drops of lemon, 3 drops of the black garlic purée, fried mint leaves and 3 small pieces of fried walnut and a few drops of charcoal oil. Cover the oyster with the flat half of the shell and hold the two halves together with a metal clamp. Set the oyster in the hot embers for 2 minutes. Paint the serving plate with a few brushstrokes of the sesame mixture and place the oyster, clamp included, on top. Remove the clamp at the table.

HIBISCUS ICE CREAM
AND BEETROOT CRUMBLE

— Serves 4. —

BERGAMOT MERINGUE

100 g bergamot juice
25 g pure albumen (egg white powder)
0.1 g green food colouring
60 g sugar
1 g powdered sumac

BEETROOT CRUMBLE

100 g cake flour
100 g ground almonds
100 g brown sugar
25 g beetroot powder
100 g butter

HIBISCUS FLOWER SYRUP

100 g sugar
500 g water
40 g dried hibiscus flowers

ICE CREAM

400 g milk
100 g cream
4 egg yolks
120 g sugar
40 g ice cream stabilizer
150 g hibiscus syrup
0.5 g red food colouring

CANTALOUPE JELLY

½ litre strained melon juice
2.5 g agar-agar

PINK PEPPERCORN OIL

100 g sunflower oil
10 g freeze-dried raspberries
10 g powdered sumac
5 g pink peppercorns

BERGAMOT MERINGUE / Beat the bergamot juice, egg white powder and colouring with an electric mixer. Once the mixture begins to rise, add the sugar in small amounts, whisking until stiff peaks have formed. Use a spatula to spread the meringue mixture thinly on a silicone mat. Dust with some sumac powder and dehydrate at 65°C for 24 hours. **BEETROOT CRUMBLE** / Use a mixer fitted with a kneading hook to create a smooth dough with the flour, ground almonds, brown sugar, beetroot powder and softened butter. Roll onto a baking tray. Bake for 15 minutes at 180°C. Remove from the oven and break up the pastry. Put it back in the oven for a further 5 minutes. Repeat the process until you have a fine, golden, crunchy mixture. **HIBISCUS FLOWER SYRUP** / Place the sugar, dried hibiscus flowers and water in a saucepan. Boil for about 30 minutes over medium heat until reduced by half. Set aside. **ICE CREAM** / Boil the milk and cream together and beat with a whisk. In a separate bowl, beat the sugar and egg yolks. Slowly pour over the milk and cream, whisking all the time. Once the custard is smooth, pour into a saucepan and heat to 84°C. **CANTALOUPE JELLY** / Mix half of the juice with the agar-agar. Boil the mixture for 1 minute, stirring all the time. Remove from the heat and add the remaining melon. Leave the mixture in the refrigerator to set. Pulverize in a blender and set aside. **PINK PEPPERCORN OIL** / Combine all the ingredients and set aside.

PLATING / To present the dish, sprinkle some crumble on the bottom of the bowl, leaving a hollow for the ice cream. Add a few drops of cantaloupe jelly and arrange some crispy bergamot meringue in an upright position around the ice cream to create volume. When serving, drizzle with some pink peppercorn oil.

A SHOT OF CHOCOLATE

— Serves 4. —

CHOCOLATE GUN

150 g cassis
15 g sugar
150 g dark chocolate (52% cocoa)
50 g cocoa butter
4 gun moulds

FLOWER BASE

100 g dark chocolate (70% cocoa)
150 g semi-whipped cream

ORANGE COULIS

50 g mango pulp
25 g cape gooseberries

RED COULIS

50 g raspberry pulp
25 g strawberry pulp

OTHER INGREDIENTS

Assorted petals and a piping bag filled
with melted chocolate

CHOCOLATE GUN / Mix the cassis with the sugar in a saucepan. Heat it just until the mixture is smooth. Allow to cool. Break the chocolate into pieces and melt. Add the cocoa butter and heat just enough to melt, making sure not to overheat. Cover the sides and base of the mould with a thin layer of chocolate. When it sets, fill the chocolate mould with the cassis syrup. Cover with more chocolate. Once the chocolate has set, remove the gun from the mould. Set aside. **FLOWER BASE** / Melt the chocolate and fold gently into the lightly whipped cream so the mixture stays firm. Pour the mixture into silicone half-sphere moulds and refrigerate 12 hours. Remove from the moulds and leave them on the plate at room temperature. **ORANGE COULIS** / Blend the mango and the cape gooseberries, strain and set aside. **RED COULIS** / Purée the berries in a food processor.

PLATING / Lay the chocolate gun on the plate and use the piping bag fitted with a fine nozzle to create some chocolate swirls. Decorate with the two sauces. Place the chocolate half sphere on the plate and cover with petals.

The aesthetics of the seventies transferred to a stuffed chocolate gun. The shot rises up from the weapon but doesn't go straight. It refuses to reach its target.

—— *A shot of chocolate* ——

NECTARINE AND SQUID VINES

— *Serves 4.* —

*SQUID INK SAUCE

1 onion
2 green Italian peppers
1 garlic clove
40 g olive oil
1 cuttlefish (300 g)
1 small tomato
½ glass red wine
2.5 l water
Salt

SQUID

12 line-caught baby squid
Grated zest of ½ lemon
1 garlic clove, finely chopped
Chopped parsley
40 g olive oil
Salt and powdered ginger

BLACK MOLE SAUCE

40 g melted dark chocolate
150 g squid ink sauce*
100 g toasted blanched almonds
100 g roasted tomatoes
100 g fried plantain
2 toasted corn tortillas
60 g roasted peanuts
20 g black sesame paste
100 g olive oil
1 dried pasilla pepper (pre-soaked, pulp only)
1 dried ancho pepper (pre-soaked, pulp only)
1 dried guajillo pepper (pre-soaked, pulp only)
200 g water
Salt and pepper

APRICOT SAUCE

50 g apricot pulp
10 g olive oil
10 g sherry vinegar
Salt and pepper

PEACH, NECTARINE AND APRICOT

½ peeled red peach
½ nectarine
½ dried apricot
4 baby peaches

OTHER INGREDIENTS

Pinch of sweet paprika
8 peach pits

SQUID INK SAUCE / Julienne the onion, peppers and garlic and sauté in the olive oil. Clean the cuttlefish and cut into pieces. Set aside the ink. When the vegetables are soft and translucent, add the cuttlefish. Sauté together for 15 minutes. Add the chopped tomato and cook until just beginning to break down. Add the wine and allow to reduce. Dilute the ink in water and add to the other ingredients. Stir well and add enough water to cover the fish. Leave to simmer for about 50 minutes over medium heat. Remove the cuttlefish and pulverize the remaining ingredients. Press the sauce through a sieve and set aside for later. Keep the cuttlefish for other recipes. **SQUID /** Separate the head and tentacles from the body and clean well. Keep the body whole. Save the ink, fins and tentacles for other recipes. Make two horizontal cuts in the baby squid without cutting through. Mix the remaining ingredients, season the squid and leave it in the mixture for 1 minute. Set aside. **BLACK MOLE SAUCE /** Pulverize all the ingredients and season. **APRICOT SAUCE /** Pulverize all the ingredients in a blender. **PEACH, NECTARINE AND APRICOT /** Clean the peach and nectarine halves and store them in oil until later. Cut the dried apricot into pieces. Cut the baby peaches in half.

PLATING / Sear the squid quickly on both sides on a flat top grill so they curl into the flower shape. Paint the plate with a little mole sauce and garnish with the remaining ingredients.

ORANGE DUCK

— Serves 4. —

MOJO SAUCE

30 g dried apricots
20 g orange juice
50 g roasted carrot
50 g roasted pumpkin
50 g toasted macadamia nuts
60 g olive oil
50 g roasted tomato
70 g sake rice wine
Juice of ½ lemon
Salt and pepper

DUCK

2 wild duck
Salt, powdered ginger and liquorice
powder

PUMPKIN RECTANGLES

100 g pumpkin
Pinch of chopped garlic
1 tbsp olive oil
Pinch of gotu kola powder
Salt and pepper

SAUCE

2 duck carcasses
3 medium onions
4 leeks
200 g olive oil
1 piece of lemon zest, finely julienned
1 piece of carrot, cut into threads
Fat rendered from the duck bones
Salt and pepper

ORANGE AND GRAPEFRUIT

½ orange
½ grapefruit
125 g honey
150 g sake
50 g white wine

CAPE GOOSEBERRIES

8 cape gooseberries
Pinch of chopped garlic
1 tbsp olive oil
Salt and pepper

FILLED DRIED APRICOT

125 g fresh duck liver
2 tbsp brandy
10 g mild, unaged white cheese
5 dried apricots
4 g powdered parsley
1 g gotu kola powder

CRISPY ONION

165 g onion
150 g onion broth
½ onion, chopped
Olive oil for frying
Salt

OTHER INGREDIENTS

A red food-safe marker

MOJO SAUCE / Pulverize all the ingredients to make a thick paste. Season with salt and pepper. Set aside. **DUCK** / Remove the duck breasts and season lightly. Generously coat with the mojo sauce and cook on a flat top grill. Set aside. Save the carcasses for the sauce. **SAUCE** / Cut up the carcasses and brown them in a pan with a little oil. Chop the vegetables and use the remaining oil to sauté them in a separate pan until golden. Strain the vegetables, add to the carcasses and sauté well. Cover with water and allow to reduce. Strain and season. Add a few drops of oil, the julienned lemon and carrot threads. Bring to a boil and set aside. **ORANGE AND GRAPEFRUIT** / Peel the orange and grapefruit. Cut into thin slices. Immerse for one minute in the honey, sake and wine mixture. Set aside. **PUMPKIN RECTANGLES** / Cut the pumpkin into rectangles and then into thin slices. Sauté in a hot pan with some oil and chopped garlic. Season and dust with gotu kola powder. **CAPE GOOSEBERRIES** / Cut the fruit in half and sauté in a hot pan with the chopped garlic. Season with salt and pepper. **FILLED DRIED APRICOT** / Chop the duck liver and sauté in a hot pan until lightly browned. Drain off the excess fat. Add the brandy and allow to sit for 5 minutes. Pulverize in a food processor with the cheese and one dried apricot. Use a piping bag to fill the dried apricots. Dust with the parsley and gotu kola powder mix. **CRISPY ONION** / Mix all the ingredients well except for the olive oil. Roll the mixture out thinly between two sheets of oven paper. Dehydrate at 60°C. Cut into pieces and fry in olive oil. Remove the oven paper and drain. Season. **PLATING** / Arrange the sliced duck breasts on a plate surrounded by the different garnishes. Use a red food-safe pen to write the name of each ingredient. Serve with a little sauce.

ALQUE QUENJE

OREJON

POMERANJA

CALA BAZA

243

CHOCOLATE ONION

— *Serves 4.* —

CHOCOLATE ONION

30 g cocoa powder
100 g sugar
50 g Cointreau
2 apples

SAUCE

100 g water
20 g cocoa
60 g sugar
1 g suma root powder
50 g Cointreau

BANANA BREAD

3 very ripe bananas
1 vanilla bean
2 eggs
65 g sugar
40 g grapeseed oil
90 g flour
8 g baking powder

OTHER INGREDIENTS

20 g sugar

CHOCOLATE ONION / Boil 20 g cocoa, 60 g sugar and the Cointreau in a saucepan for 1 minute. Allow to cool. Use an apple peeler to cut two 2-metre-long strips of apple. Spread them out and sprinkle with 40 g sugar and 10 g cocoa. Roll the strips up to create onion shapes. Cut each horizontally to create four halves and place in the liquid until ready to use. **SAUCE** / Boil all the ingredients in a saucepan for 5 minutes. Cool and set aside. **BANANA BREAD** / Peel the bananas and mash with a fork. Add the seeds from the vanilla bean. Keep the bean for other recipes. Beat the eggs and sugar until they reach the ribbon stage. Then combine the mixture with the mashed banana. Next, add the grapeseed oil. In a separate bowl, mix the flour with the baking powder and fold into the banana and egg mixture. Pour the batter into a baking tin and bake for 18 minutes at 180°C. Remove from the tin and cut into 2 × 2 cm cubes. Dehydrate at 55°C. Keep in the dehydrator until ready to use.

PLATING / Coat one side of the chocolate onion with sugar and caramelize well on a frying pan. To serve, place three cubes of dried banana cake next to the chocolate onion. Sauce sparingly.

HONEYMEAD AND FRACTAL FLUID

— Serves 4. —

CRUMBLE BASE

250 g flour
125 g softened butter
1 egg
1 egg yolk
1 tbsp water
100 g sugar
1.5 g tandoori masala
1.5 g sweet paprika
0.5 g cochineal food colouring
20 g blue Curaçao
10 g apple liqueur

LEMON STRUCTURES

150 g lemon juice
Peel of 2 lemons
2 eggs
2 egg yolks
100 g butter
50 g liquid glucose
50 g milk
100 g sugar

LEMON STRUCTURE EXTERIOR

200 g cocoa butter
3 g sweet paprika
0.5 g cochineal food colouring

MEAD

500 g water
100 g honey
2 star anise
100 g birch sugar
1.5 g Xantana

REACTIVE COMPONENT

10 g vodka
1.7 g cochineal food colouring
5 g water
2 g sugar

OTHER INGREDIENTS

Bitter cocoa powder

CRUMBLE BASE / Knead ingredients together (except the Curaçao and apple liqueur) and leave in the refrigerator for 1 hour. Roll out the dough on an oven sheet and bake for 80 minutes at 140ºC. Allow to cool and crumble it completely. Add the Curaçao and the apple liqueur to 150 g of the crumble. **LEMON STRUCTURES** / Mix all ingredients together. Bring the mixture to a boil, pour into square-shaped silicone moulds and freeze. Once firm, cut in half and create curvy edges. Store in the freezer. **LEMON STRUCTURE EXTERIOR** / Melt the cocoa butter only to 50ºC. Mix in the paprika and cochineal colouring. Using a hypodermic needle, bathe the frozen lemon structures with the liquid, just enough to create a film on the exterior. Allow to cool in the refrigerator. **MEAD** / Boil the water and honey together. Infuse the liquid with the star anise for 5 minutes. Let cool. Place the remaining ingredients in a professional blender and pulverize. Let the mead sit in the refrigerator for 6 hours to remove any air bubbles. **REACTIVE COMPONENT** / Mix the ingredients together.

PLATING / Sprinkle the lemon structures with cocoa powder so that they have a rusty colour. Place the crumble base on a flat dish or slate and arrange 2 lemon structures per person. Pour 50 g of the mead into a separate dish. At the table, pour the reactive mixture over the top using a teaspoon to produce a fractal reaction.

Sometimes investigation winks at fate. Discovering how a fractal is created was the magic that made the research possible. It happens once in a lifetime. But the key is to be there to grab it.

—— Honeymead and fractal fluid ——

TEAM ARZAK 2018

YOLANDA ARIAS
CRISTINA ARROYO
ELENA ARZAK
JUAN MARI ARZAK
MARTA ARZAK
JAVIER AVILEO
AVILES ADOLFO
BORJA AZCARATE
ITZIAR BANDRES
RUTH BAZO
KONTXI BEOBIDE
JAIME BUSTO
DIEGO CALVO
MARGA CANTERO
MIKEL CORCUERA
ISIS CRUZ
ANNY CUEVAS
MARIA EGUIA
TERESA EGUIA
MAITE ESPINA
MARISA FERNANDEZ
CESAR GARNACHO
PACA GARRIDO
DAVID GONZÁLEZ
ION GUTIÉRREZ
XABIER GUTIÉRREZ
JOSÉ MANUEL HERNÁNDEZ
JUAN JESÚS HOYOS
OLHA HURTOVA
ESTHER IBÁÑEZ
ASIER IRIGOIEN
TXON JAÑEZ DE LA FUENTE
LILI KONOVAL
MANUEL LAMOSA

Mª JOSÉ LAZKANO
LÓPEZ LUIS
NICOMEDES LÓPEZ
YOLANDA LÓPEZ
MAIALEN LOYOLA
AMAIA MASE
ANYELA MÉNDEZ
KAREN MÉNDEZ
PACO MESA
AINHOA MIRASOLAIN
MARTA MIRASOLAIN
MAITE ORTEGA
MARIBI OTAEGUI
LARA PÉREZ
LUCIA PÉREZ
Mª CARMEN PESQUEIRA
RAMÓN PORTU
GABRIELLA RANELLI
MÓNICA RICO
Mª JOSE RODRÍGUEZ
MARIANO RODRÍGUEZ
ENARA SÁENZ DE JÁUREGUI
MAITE SANTESTEBAN
MIKEL SORAZU
ALICIA TADEO
KEI TAKAHASI
YAJAIRA TEJADA
ERIKA TOLA
PILAR UGARTEMENDIA
PIO UGARTEMENDIA
KARMELE URRESTARAZU
RUT VALDERREY
CYNTHIA YABER
IGOR ZALAKAIN

249

From the Arzak family we would like to thank all the people who at one point have been part of the team, collaborators and suppliers. Your effort, patience and dedication have without a doubt been the most important for restaurant Arzak to be where it is.

We do not want to forget our clientele as well as the media that allow us to spread our gastronomy around the world.

Eskerrik asko.

Acknowledgements

This English language edition published in 2020 by
Grub Street
4 Rainham Close
London
SW11 6SS

Email: food@grubstreet.co.uk
Web: www.grubstreet.co.uk
Twitter: @grub_street
Facebook: Grub Street Publishing

First published in Spanish by Editorial Planeta, S. A., 2018
© Editorial Planeta, S. A. 2018
© Bainet, S.L.
© Juan Mari y Elena Arzak
Text: Gabriella Ranelli, Xabier Gutiérrez & Igor Zalakain
Photography: Sara Santos / except:
Pages 6, 28, 40, 41, 42, 44, 45, 46, 47, 48, 61, 62, 94,
95, 97, 98, 99, 100, 101, 104, 105, 167 / Mikel Alonso
Pages 4, 5, 143, 151, 159, 174, 190, 215, 221, 222,
231, 239 / Diaporama Estudio
Pages 127, 246, 247 / Sergio Coimbra
Photographic retouching/ Bjorn Badetti

A CIP catalogue record for this book is available from the
British Library.

ISBN 978-1-911621-86-7

Printed and bound by Hussar Books in Poland

ARZA-K